Skin Deep

Marie-Louise von Franz, Honorary Patron

**Studies in Jungian Psychology
by Jungian Analysts**

Daryl Sharp, Founder and General Editor Emeritus

SKIN DEEP

Manifestations of the Unconscious in Everyday Life

Brian Mayo and Patricia Brannigan

We dedicate this book to our spouses, Lucia and Doug, who have been very supportive throughout this book writing venture.

Library and Archives Canada Cataloguing in Publication

Mayo, Brian, and Brannigan, Patricia, author.
Skin Deep:
Manifestations of the Unconscious in Everyday
Life / Brian Mayo and Patricia Brannigan

(Studies in Jungian psychology by Jungian analysts; 147)

Includes bibliographical references.

ISBN 9781738738519

1. Tattooing—Decision making—Psychological aspects.
I. Jungian psychology. II. Subconsciousness.

GT2345 .M39 2024   391.6/5—dc23

Copyright © 2024 by Brian Mayo and Patricia Brannigan.
All rights reserved.

INNER CITY BOOKS
21 Milroy Crescent Toronto ON M1C 4B6
Canada
416-927-0355 www.innercitybooks.net

Founder and General Editor Emeritus: Daryl Sharp
Honorary Patron: Marie-Louise von Franz
Publisher and General Editor: Scott Milligen
IT and Production Manager: Sharpconnections.com

INNER CITY BOOKS was founded in 1980 to promote the understanding and practical application of the work of C.G. Jung.

Cover design by David Sharp. Cover art by David Anderson.

Printed and bound in Canada by Rapido Livres Books.

Acknowledgements

This project relating to the tattoo would not have been completed without significant contributions from others. In the early stages of the project, Perry Cheung's expertise as a lawyer was instrumental in drafting the Research Study Participant Agreement. Perry also made considerable contributions towards assisting the authors in recruiting participants for the project. The exploration of tattoos would not have been possible without the gracious participation of the ten individuals. Stacey Jenkins, a Registered Psychotherapist as well as a Jungian colleague, provided the necessary information that connected the authors with the book's illustrator, David Anderson. David's illustrations of the tattoos are done with skill and accuracy. The cover he designed reflects his originality and considerable artistic talent. Terilynn Graham Freedman, RP, another Jungian colleague, provided invaluable editorial input to the project despite a challenging workload. The authors offer our heartfelt gratitude to each of the aforementioned individuals.

Contents

Introduction 7

Psychology and the Tattoo 11

Mark 15

Mary 31

Joseph 50

Sophie 80

Summary 118

List of Tattoos 119

References 120

Introduction

"Everything in the unconscious seeks outward manifestation, and the personality too desires to evolve out of its unconscious conditions and to experience itself as a whole."[1]
- Carl Jung

It has been about one hundred years since Carl Jung outlined his understanding of the psyche, yet there has been little research in psychiatry and the medical field that attempts to utilize his perspective of the psyche. This omission is troubling but not surprising. As Marie-Louise von Franz suggests, there seems to be a stumbling block of sorts for many people, both layperson and professional specialist alike, for grasping the reality of the unconscious psyche and the role it plays in an individual life.[2] Most people generally understand Jung's description of the ego as the reference point or centre of consciousness.[3] Many also understand Jung's description of the personal unconscious with its feeling-toned complexes. However, when Jung extends his description of the unconscious psyche by positing a collective unconscious, only a minority of people seem to really comprehend what he proposes. Even for those that accept and understand Jung's notion of the collective unconscious, it is an even smaller minority who fully understand that the collective unconscious is an omnipresent dimension of the unconscious psyche, which influences the conscious personality in an ongoing, dynamic way. In North America and European countries, this may be attributable in part to the current prevailing *Weltanschauung* in academic and medical fields, where research focuses primarily on the conscious personality and not the unconscious aspect of the psyche. From a Jungian

---

[1] C.G. Jung, *Memories, Dreams, Reflections*, ed. Aniela Jaffe (London: Fontana Press, 1993), p. 3.
[2] Marie-Louise von Franz, *C.G. Jung - His Myth in Our Time* (Toronto: Inner City Books, 1998), p. 11.
[3] C.G. Jung, *Psychological Types*. Collected Works, Vol. 6 (Princeton: Princeton University Press, 1972), p. 425.

perspective, the ego develops or emerges from birth out of its unconscious foundation. (An elucidation of some of Jung's most relevant concepts is found here in the chapter, Psychology and the Tattoo).

Despite Jung's model of the psyche being under-utilized by academia and the medical field, it has the potential to assist people in understanding the complexity of the inner life of the psyche, in all its manifestations. The intention of this book is to explore the applicability of Jung's model of the psyche with regard to understanding everyday life and behaviour. To accomplish this intention, we will investigate a cultural practice and phenomenon found throughout the world: the tattoo.

The symbols and images tattooed on individual bodies, examined through a Jungian lens, suggest how the image, the ego, and the unconscious relate and are psychologically interconnected. Part of the symbol's meaning derives from the outside world while another part owes its meaning to the inner world of the psyche. Following Jung's lead, we will trace the psychological story contained within the symbols and images discussed in these sample case studies.

The word tattoo originated in recent centuries, whereas the practice itself dates back much further. As defined by the *Concise Oxford Dictionary*, a tattoo is "an indelible mark or pattern made on a person's skin by inserting pigments in punctures."[4] The word derives from the Tahitian *tau-tau* or *tatu*, which means "to mark." The word returned to Europe with Captain Cook in 1771, when his narratives of his travels to Tahiti mention a process called *tattaw*. For the first time the word "tattooing" is used.[5]

No one can say, with any assurance, where or when tattooing started. A review of the literature on the topic suggests that various cultures, spontaneously and independent of outside influence, began to tattoo

---

[4] The *Concise Oxford Dictionary of Current English*, eighth edition, ed. R. E. Allen (New York: Oxford University Press, 1990) p. 1250.
[5] George Burchett and Peter Leighton, *Memoirs of a Tattooist* (London: Pan Books, 1960) p. 19.

whereas some began to tattoo only after coming into contact with the practice via other cultures. One thing is certain, tattooing has been found to occur in practically every area of the world. A conservative estimate would be that tattooing predates recorded history by several thousand years.

Examples of books written about the tattoo include John Gray's *I Love Mom - An Irreverent History of the Tattoo*, and Amy Krakow's *The Total Tattoo Book*. Many of them mention the multiple reasons people and cultures tattoo. Some of the reasons include: 1) utilization in religious rituals; 2) utilization in important rites of passage; 3) the branding of slaves and criminals; 4) decorative and identity enhancement; 5) medicinal purposes; 6) inclusion, i.e. various trades (Japanese firefighters) and criminal gangs (Japanese yakuza); 7) mnemonic devices; 8) devotion; 9) the bolstering of self-esteem; 10) images of recognition by the gatekeepers in the afterlife; 11) fun and enjoyment; 12) symbols/images of a personal nature.

The tattoo has undergone a renaissance in Western culture in recent years. Historically, in Western culture the tattoo has been viewed largely as a phenomenon that takes place on the proverbial "other side of the tracks," in the neglected, low income and socially marginalized parts of communities. However, a shift has taken place within Western society and the tattoo has crossed over the tracks and is found in all segments of society. In the 1930s, literature reports that approximately 10% of the American population is tattooed.[6] In 2018, Joe Pierre, M.D., wrote an article in *Psychology Today* entitled "Tattoos as Windows to the Psyche - The Psychology of Skin Art." He reports that 30% of the American population is tattooed and almost 50% of those are between the ages of 18-35.[7]

In investigating the tattoo, we enlisted ten participants with tattoos. Each was interviewed about their personal and psychological histories. All provided photos of their tattoos. To protect the

---

[6] Amy Krakow, *Total Tattoo Book*, Warner Books, 1994, pp. 4-6.
[7] Joe Pierre, Tattoos as Windows to the Psyche: The Psychology of Skin Art. *Psychology Today*. (New York: Sussex Publishers, February 1, 2018).

confidentiality of the participants we agreed to include artistic renderings of their tattoos in the book rather than actual photos.

It is our hypothesis that the phenomenon under investigation exemplifies areas of life where the unconscious can be seen to manifest. When one enters the confines of a tattoo shop with its array of imagery on the wall one forms the impression that tattoos have something to do with the depths of the human psyche, namely, the collective unconscious with its archetypal foundation outlined by Jung. This book is the result of our exploration of the psychological impressions related to tattoos.

Psychology and the Tattoo

"I inquire, I do not assert; I do not here determine anything with final assurance; I conjecture, try, compare, attempt, ask..."[8]
- Motto to Christian Knorr von Rosenroth (Quoted on the title page of *The Psychology of the Transference* by Carl Jung.)

From the outset, we emphasize that this investigation of the tattoo is in no way an attempt to make value judgements about participants' tattoos. It was a pleasure to meet and interview the diverse participants of this small investigation. Our intent is to try and understand the tattoo from the perspective of Jungian psychology, as at this point, there is limited published research on the tattoo. We have found this somewhat puzzling, as tattoo images have been found all over the world for thousands of years and Jungians' interest in symbols and images is their supposed bailiwick. Although this investigation does not follow the rigorous scientific methodology of some formal studies, it does make a serious attempt to understand the psychology behind the tattoo.

In talking to the participants of this investigation, a common refrain we heard was the experience of an *impulse* to get a tattoo. Some of the participants felt this impulse to get a tattoo and acquired one that very day. Others, upon experiencing the impulse to acquire a tattoo, would start a process, thinking about what image they would select and taking a month or two before getting the tattoo. On one occasion, a participant knew the image they wanted tattooed on their body and waited four years before acquiring it! However, in all cases, the decision to get the tattoo began with an impulse.

The impulse to get a tattoo varied from individual to individual. For one participant, the impulse did not recur after getting the initial tattoo. Many of the participants did get additional tattoos after the

---

[8] C.G. Jung, *The Practice of Psychotherapy*. Collected Works, Vol. 16 (Princeton: Princeton University Press, 1975) p. 163.

initial one and planned to get more in the future. Several indicated that they experienced the impulse to get another tattoo immediately after getting the initial tattoo. Many of the participants described the experience of a craving to get additional tattoos after the initial one. Some described getting additional tattoos as addictive in nature. Where does this impulse to get a tattoo originate? This was a question that begged for an answer.

Jung defines the psyche as "the totality of all psychic processes, conscious as well as unconscious."[9] He describes the ego as the centre of consciousness which "seems to arise in the first place from the collision between the somatic factor and the environment, and once established as a subject, it goes on developing from further collisions with the outer world and the inner."[10] However, it is important to note that the impulse to tattoo does not originate with the ego. The ego experiences the impulse. The impulsion towards certain activities, Jung ascribes to the instinct. He elaborates further: "The impulsion can come from an inner or outer stimulus which triggers off the mechanism of instinct psychically."[11] So, following Jung's understanding, the impulse to tattoo originates when outer and inner stimuli experienced by the ego trigger the instinctual component of the psyche. When the impulse becomes a craving or is addictive in nature, it is experienced more as a compulsion. Whether an individual experiences an impulse or a compulsion to get a tattoo, the impulse or compulsion originates from the instinctual, unconscious foundation of the psyche.

As the impulse originates from the instinctual and unconscious aspect of the psyche, a few remarks are required to explain Jung's understanding of the unconscious psyche. Jung outlines the unconscious aspect of the psyche as consisting of a personal unconscious and a collective unconscious. He describes the personal unconscious as consisting, for the most part, of feeling-toned complexes, while the contents of the collective unconscious are the

---

[9] C.G. Jung, *Psychological Types*. p. 463.
[10] C.G. Jung, *Aion: Researches into the Phenomenology of the Self*. Collected Works, Vol. 9, Part 2 (Princeton: Princeton University Press, 1968) p. 5.
[11] C.G. Jung, *Psychological Types*, p. 451.

archetypes.[12] Though the two layers of the unconscious and their contents can be conceptually differentiated, experientially, the one rests on and develops out of the other. A personal complex ultimately develops out of the archetypal foundation of the psyche. Jung defines the feeling-toned complex as follows:

> In my studies on the phenomena of association I have shown that there are certain constellations of psychic contents grouped around feeling-toned contents, which I have called "complexes." The feeling-toned content, the complex, consists of a nuclear element and a large number of secondarily constellated associations. The nuclear element consists of two components: first, a factor determined by experience and causally related to the environment; second, a factor innate in the individual's character and determined by his disposition.[13]

As mentioned, Jung defines the contents of the collective unconscious as archetypes or primordial images. Unlike the personal unconscious, the contents of the collective unconscious are impersonal in nature. The archetypal contents that form the structural foundation of the unconscious psyche are common to every individual, much the same as every person has a similar anatomical structure. Jung considers the archetypes to be the blueprint of everything in the human psyche.[14]

In order to better understand the impulse to get a tattoo, it is necessary to trace the impulse back to its origins in the collective unconscious aspect of the psyche. Jung describes the archetype by using the simile of the spectrum of visible light. At each end of the spectrum, there are invisible wavelengths of light, which are analogous to the unconscious workings of the psyche. There are colours we can't see with our eyes, but they are there just the same. As unconscious contents reach the threshold of consciousness, they become accessible to our awareness, the same way only certain wavelengths

---

[12] C.G. Jung, *The Archetypes and The Collective Unconscious*. Collected Works, Vol. 9, Part 1 (Princeton: Princeton University Press, 1975) p. 4.
[13] C.G. Jung, *The Structure and Dynamics of the Psyche*. Collected Works, Vol. 8. (Princeton: Princeton University Press, 1972) pp. 10-11.
[14] C.G. Jung, *Psychological Types*, pp. 443-447.

in the visible spectrum can be seen as colours by our eyes. Jung used this simile to explain the archetype as embodying two aspects, one being the "ultraviolet" aspect, the other being the "infrared" aspect. The ultraviolet aspect of the archetype has to do with typical modes of apprehension, namely, the meaning contained within the archetype. The infrared aspect has to do with typical modes of action, of instinctual responses connected to an archetype. The image is the ultraviolet representation of dynamic instinct, whereas the infrared aspect is the dynamic instinct itself associated with the archetype. As outlined by Jung, just as the colours on a spectrum have no distinct separating lines between them, the ultraviolet and infrared aspects of the archetype are seamlessly and mysteriously interconnected within the archetype as if on a sliding scale.[15]

Mark, Mary, Joseph, and Sophie. All four names are pseudonyms to protect the identities of the participants.

---

[15] Barbara Hannah, *The Archetypal Symbolism of Animals* (Wilmette, Illinois: Chiron Publications, 2006) pp.134-144.

Mark

To illustrate how the impulse to get a tattoo can be understood from a practical perspective, we have chosen an example case: the initial tattoo of a participant we identify as "Mark" (a pseudonym). At age twenty-two, Mark decided to get his first tattoo. His grandfather, who had lived in the family home for ten years, passed away. After his death, Mark experienced an impulse to get a tattoo to honour what his grandfather meant to him. Mark selected his grandfather's family crest to memorialize him (see Tattoo #1 below). Mark embellished the family crest by placing it upon a warrior's shield with two swords crossing in the shape of an X behind the shield. Mark, who had a total of six tattoos at the time of the interview, said he puts a lot of thought into a tattoo before settling upon a final version of a chosen image. He stated this initial tattoo has multiple reference points in his memory. He had always been interested in knights and the warrior spirit, so decided to include a shield and swords in his first tattoo to express this interest. The tattoo was placed in the middle of his upper back over his spine, between the shoulder blades. Mark was not certain why he chose to put his first tattoo on his back. He suggested that the placement may be related to the fact that he was not fully committed to "the tattoo thing" at the time he acquired the initial tattoo. Later, when he was committed fully to acquiring tattoos, they were placed on more visible areas of the body.

Tattoo 1

Before elucidating the psychology behind Mark's initial tattoo, it is important to provide context relevant to understanding it. At the very time Mark was acquiring the tattoo, he was making decisions to change his life for the better. Mark, who was thirty-five at the time of the interview, remembers experiencing a persistent sense of shyness as he was growing up. Deep down, he realized his shyness did not really represent him as a person; therefore, at the age of twenty-two, he decided to make dramatic changes in his thinking and behaviour in an effort to become a more outgoing and self-confident individual. He implemented this change by volunteering, doing public speaking, and working towards entering a profession that necessitated adopting a professional persona of composure and self-confidence. His first tattoo was a memorable experience for him. The pain of getting a tattoo over the spinal column left him with the memory of having gone through a meaningful experience.

As mentioned, the impulse for Mark's initial tattoo was related to the death of his grandfather. A conscious aspect of the initial tattoo was that Mark wanted it to memorialize the memory of his grandfather. He did this by incorporating his grandfather's family crest in the tattoo on his back. Another conscious aspect was his inclusion of the knight and warrior spirits, embellishing the family crest with swords and a shield. Both aspects of the tattoo were connected to a persona that the ego created and with which the ego was identified. One aspect of the persona component of the initial tattoo was Mark's identification with his deceased grandfather. The other aspect was his identification with the persona of the knight and warrior spirits. The *persona* is a term adopted and defined by Jung to designate the part of the personality that is created by the ego to assist its relationship to the outside world. It is like a mask a person adopts. This mask depends on the social context and assists the ego in relating to a situation. The persona is the version of the ego that a person wants to share with the outer world in a given context.[16] Psychologically, Mark's initial tattoo reflected the challenges he experienced in transitioning to a new more self-confident persona, as he was not yet fully comfortable exposing the tattoo with people, for example, in the workplace. It is noteworthy that the part of the tattoo that was visible when he was wearing an undershirt, which he did frequently, was the two sword handles sticking out. When this partially exposed image became a catalyst for conversation, as it often did, Mark could choose to share as much about the sword and the storyline associated with it as he saw fit. Hence, from a persona perspective, the placement of the initial tattoo suggested that at the age of twenty-two, Mark was in the early stages of transitioning to a new, more self-confident persona.

When discussing the persona, one is essentially making comments about the status of the ego, as the persona is created by the ego. Therefore, the difficulty in transitioning to the new self-confident persona suggested that the ego's confidence was somewhat labile and intermittent at the age of twenty-two. Mark hoped his self-confidence and inner sense of composure would become more of a psychological constant in time, as he was committed to making positive psychological changes. His ego's identification with the code of the knight and with the warrior's spirit was something the ego was aware of as it strove in its quest to fight for a more psychologically

---

[16] C.G. Jung, *Psychological Types*, p. 465.

composed inner and outer life. Also, it must be pointed out that the persona not only assists the ego to relate to the outer world, it also functions as a shield, as a means of protecting and defending the ego. Therefore, the grandfather's family crest, centred on the warrior's shield with two crossing swords behind it, was the ego's attempt to defend both itself and the memory of the grandfather. The defense aspect of the persona is a work in progress and reflects the need of the persona to protect the ego from the slings and arrows of everyday life.

Growing up, Mark's shyness and lack of self-confidence, his inner insecurity, can be described as a feeling-toned complex influencing the ego from the personal unconscious. The initial impulse to get a tattoo symbolizes a compensatory response to this feeling-toned complex within the personal unconscious by the central regulating archetype of the collective unconscious, the Self, to address and rectify the ego's chronic insecurity. According to Jung, the Self is a hypothetical postulate based on empirical experience. It is the centreing and ordering archetype within the total psyche, as the ego is the centre of the conscious personality. Thus, the Self is the supreme authority within the psyche, while the ego is subordinate to it. [17] As the Self operates out of the depths of the collective unconscious, it has an irrepresentable and transcendental component. Nonetheless, it manifests empirically in the motifs of dreams, myths and fairytales in "the figure of the supra-ordinate personality, such as a king, hero, prophet, saviour, etc., or in the form of a totality symbol, such as the circle, square, *quadrata circuli*, cross, etc."[18] The Self manifests empirically in images combining light and shadow and hence as a totality symbol in which the opposites are united. Symbols of the Self often carry a distinct numinosity. [19] Jung describes the numinous as a "gripping emotionality" with a spiritual characteristic.[20]

---

[17] Edward Edinger, *Ego and Archetype* (Boston: Shambala, 1992) p. 3.
[18] C.G. Jung, *Psychological Types*, p. 460.
[19] Ibid., pp. 460-461.
[20] C.G. Jung, *Letters,* 2nd vol. 1951-1961 (Princeton Univ. Press, 1975) p.517.

In the tattoo on Mark's back, the archetype of the Self manifests in the symbol of the shield and the crossing swords behind it. Both the shield and the crossing swords symbolize mandalas. Mark would be unaware of the mandala connotations of the tattoo and their association with the archetype of the Self. Jung spent much of his professional research investigating the psychological implications of the mandala. The word *mandala* means "orb or circle with a connotation of magic."[21] The magic circle has an apotropaic effect meaning "a way to ward off," or "hold off."[22] However, as Jung discovered, the mandala does not solely refer to the circle but also to the square. In his American lectures in 1936-7 on "Dream Symbols of the Individuation Process," Jung outlines the significance of the mandala symbolism in physicist Wolfgang Pauli's dreams. He describes how the mandala may show itself symbolically in a circle or square or in a squaring of the circle. He summarizes the meaning of the mandala at the beginning of a lecture on October 17, 1937, where he states "it is the circle, the rotation, the circulation, the circumambulation, the center, the middle; also the square and the four, because the square and the circle always belong together."[23]

According to Jung, "the symbol of the mandala is always an attempt at self-cure..."[24] He also states that the conscious and the unconscious aspects of the psyche come together in the mandala, in the square, which acts as a protective *temenos* for individuation.[25] The mandala appears when an individual is experiencing a sense of disorientation, confusion and chaos. As such, it brings orientation, order and meaning.[26] At twenty-two, as Mark's ego attempted to transition to a more self-confident persona, his longstanding insecurity and sense of shyness prompted the Self to issue a compensatory impulse, of protection, support and healing,

---

[21] C.G. Jung, *Dream Analysis: Notes on the Seminar Given in 1928-30*. William McGuire, ed. (Princeton: Princeton University Press, 1984) p. 120.
[22] C.G. Jung, *Dream Symbols of the Individuation Process* (Princeton: Princeton University Press, 2019) p. 88.
[23] Ibid., p. 243.
[24] Ibid., p. 224.
[25] Ibid., p. 195.
[26] Marie-Louise von Franz, *C.G. Jung - His Myth in Our Time*, p. 150.

symbolized by the mandalas of the shield and the intercrossing swords.

The intercrossing swords not only symbolize a mandala, they also symbolize the archetype of the warrior. While the mandala symbolizes the protective, ordering and healing aspect of the Self, the warrior aspect of the sword symbolizes the fighting spirit that the ego needs to integrate if it is to fulfill its goal of becoming more confident. From a young age, Mark's imagination had been stirred by anything to do with knights and warriors. He identified with the code of the knight, to live a strong and just life helping others. His ambition, at this time, was to enter a profession dedicated towards defending justice and the safety and wellbeing of others. On the psychological level, the code of the knight, like that of Percival in his quest for the Grail in the King Arthur legend, symbolizes the process of individuation.

We have traced the origin of the impulse to the archetypes within the collective unconscious and suggested the archetypes activated and influencing Mark's ego to be the archetypes of the warrior and the Self. While Mark was aware of some of the psychological aspects of the initial tattoo, such as the warrior connotation of the shield and sword, he was unaware of the archetypal dimension of the tattoo with its implications. Interestingly, the unconscious dimension of the initial tattoo is contained within the symbolism of the sword. In *The Grail Legend*, Emma Jung and Marie-Louise von Franz discuss the psychological symbolism of the sword. They describe the sword as a masculine weapon which connotes strength and power, serving to overcome hostile opponents. The sword is often very closely associated with the identity of its owner, as was Arthur's sword, Excalibur. "As a cutting weapon it serves to separate or, metaphorically, to differentiate, so it can stand for the mind, especially the intellect or understanding intelligence, of whose incisive quality we speak. As the sword of Justice, it also signifies judgement, wrath and vengeance."[27] They also speak of the sword as sometimes symbolizing the "divinity concealed in man," as having

---

[27] Emma Jung and Marie-Louise von Franz, *The Grail Legend* (Boston: Sigo Press, 1986) p. 80.

symbolic associations to the alchemists' "divine water" and the philosopher's stone. As such, "the sword signifies that life-urge which leads to the recognition of the Self."[28] Also, if one were to look at the handles of Mark's two intercrossing swords, one would come to realize, as Jung points out, that "the sword has always symbolized the cross."[29] Mark's intercrossing swords did form a cross.

It is important to remember the analogy of the two aspects of the archetype: namely, the ultraviolet and the infrared. We explained previously that the ultraviolet has to do with the mode of apprehension, or the meaning symbolized by the archetypal image. Mark valued healthy debate. He enjoyed the back-and-forth of people discussing various perspectives, of trying to develop the mind. Having said that, it was unlikely Mark associated the symbol of the sword with psychological discrimination. Rather, he probably associated the sword with the conscious mental quest of fighting for the good in life, and with defending himself and others from injustice. Though he had long identified with the questing spirit of the knight, he would not be consciously aware that by identifying with the sword, he had chosen a symbol that represents psychological discrimination and a life-urge that led to a recognition of the Self. As mentioned, the two swords intercrossing behind the shield form a cross. The cross itself is a mandala. While it is neither a circle or a square, it is a mandala with historic apotropaic associations through its power to protect and ward off evil. The point where the two crosses connect symbolizes the epicentre of the psyche. In consciousness, it is the ego; within the unconscious, it is the Self. The sword is the life-urge within the ego that connects it to the Self. It is the mode of apprehension aspect — the meaning — contained within the ultraviolet aspect of the archetypal image that Mark would need to become more conscious. This viewpoint gains resonance when considering another aspect of the sword symbol: number.

Jung believed that ultimately all life, psyche and matter, is connected in some inconceivable way. He uses the term *unus mundus* to refer to this "one world." He also came to believe that the

---

[28] Ibid., p. 89.
[29] C.G. Jung, *Dream Analysis: Notes on the Seminar Given in 1928-30*, p. 337.

interconnectedness of psyche and matter manifests in what he describes as synchronistic events.

> In his paper on synchronicity Jung stresses the point that since the physical and and the psychic realms coincide within the synchronistic event, there must be somewhere or somehow a unitarian reality — one reality of the physical and psychic realms to which he gave the Latin expression *unus mundus*, the one world, a concept which already existed in the minds of some mediaeval philosophers. This world, Jung says, we cannot visualize, and it completely transcends our conscious grasp. We can only conclude, or assume, that there is somewhere such a reality, a psycho-physical reality we could call it, which sporadically manifests in the synchronistic event. Later, in *Mysterium Coniunctionis*, he says that the mandala is the inner psychic equivalent of the *unus mundus*.[30]

Following the hypothesis Jung puts forth in "Synchronicity: An Acausal Connecting Principle," he increasingly came to believe that all natural numbers, i.e., 1,2,3,4,5 etc., underlie and constitute the ordering principle of the archetypes and the "key impulse" behind archetypal images. Jung held the belief that number is a mysterious link connecting psyche and matter.[31] Toward the end of his life, when he no longer had the energy to tackle major research with regard to numbers, he wrote a few notes and handed them to von Franz and requested she follow up on his hypothesis. The book *Number and Time* is the culmination of von Franz's years of research trying to understand the psychological aspect of numbers.[32] Regarding Jung's thinking about numbers, he was strongly influenced by the Chinese perspective which he encountered in Wilhelm's (translation of) *The Secret of the Golden Flower*, and study of the I Ching. Unlike the western scientific perspective, which heavily emphasizes the quantitative aspect of number, the Chinese consider the qualitative aspect of number as central. Von Franz describes how the Chinese

---

[30] Marie-Louise von Franz, *On Divination and Synchronicity-The Psychology of Meaningful Chance* (Toronto: Inner City Books, 1980) p. 98.
[31] Marie-Louise von Franz, *Number and Time* (Evanston: Northwestern University Press, 1974) pp. 9-10.
[32] Ibid., ix.

perspective is directed towards what she calls "field thinking," at the centre of which is time.[33] They believed that the universe has a numerical rhythm, and that "The underlying numerical order of eternity is called the *Ho-tou*, a mandala and also a cross."[34] This Chinese perspective coincides with Jung's understanding of the archetypal structure of the collective unconscious.

The number two and the number four figure prominently in Mark's back tattoo design, from a qualitative perspective. Jung has stated that the number one was not the first number; rather, the first number was two, and with it, multiplicity and reality manifested.[35] Von Franz spoke to the qualitative aspect of number two in the following:

> But the number two not only appears to form the basis for our possible range of perceptions on the physical level; it also applies to the psychic level. Besides its specific relation to the structural binary basis of matter, two possesses an equally important relationship to the so-called threshold phenomena of consciousness. Identical duplications of objects in dreams, for instance, or in myths, point to the fact that a content is just beginning to reach the threshold of consciousness as a recognizable entity, taking the first step, as it were, toward manifestation.[36]

What this means with regard to the two swords is that the multiple meanings, previously mentioned as associated with the symbol, were now approaching the threshold of consciousness. The two swords suggested the time was ripe for Mark to become psychologically conscious of the ultraviolet aspect of the meanings of the archetypal image associated with the sword. This means that Mark, like Percival in the legend of the Grail, needs to ask the relevant question, for instance, "What is the meaning of the sword?" and "Who does it serve?". From the perspective of depth psychology, the sword symbolizes psychological discrimination and the life-urge within the ego that connects it to the Self. As such, the sword serves the ego in

---

[33] Marie-Louise von Franz, *On Divination and Synchronicity - The Psychology of Meaningful Chance*, p. 8.
[34] Ibid., p.14.
[35] Marie-Louise von Franz, *Number and Time*, p. 97.
[36] Ibid., pp. 91-92.

its quest for positive transformation which includes increased self-confidence, maturity and a sense of being in touch with the Self.

The other number related to Mark's tattoo is the number four. Jung indicated that the qualitative aspect of the number four had to do with the archetypal potential of the individual for psychological wholeness. The number four is connected both to the square and to the cross. There were also four individual images on Mark's family crest. Jung speaks about the significance of the cross and the number four in his dream seminar of 1928-30:

> Yes, it seems to have been one of the most original intuitions of man that the right form to express the source of mana would be the cross. Plato says in Timaeus that when the Demiourgos created the world, he divided it into four parts, and then he sewed them together again, four seams in the form of the cross. Here the origin of the world is connected with the sign of the cross, the original act of giving life. Pythagoras, who was earlier than Plato, says the fundamental number is four, the tetraktys, which was considered by the Pythagoreans as a mystical unity...
>
> My idea is that the symbol of the cross does not originate from any external form, but from an endopsychic vision of the primitive man. The peculiar nature of the vision expresses, as nearly as man can grasp it, the essential quality of life's energy as it appeared not only in him but also in all his objects. It is an absolutely irrational fact to me that vital energy should have anything to do with the cross or with the number four. I don't know why it is perceived in such a form; I only know that the cross has always meant mana or life-power.[37]

The number four, associated with the archetypal potential for psychological wholeness, is corroborated by Jung's hypothesis of the four psychological functions, i.e., thinking, feeling, sensation, and intuition. The four psychological functions, when developed and differentiated by the ego, provide it with the possibility of approximating the experience of wholeness. The symmetry, order

---

[37] C.G. Jung, *Dream Analysis: Notes on the Seminar Given in 1928-30*, pp. 363-364.

and meaning associated with the qualitative aspect of the number four is the archetypal foundation underlying this developmental possibility. That Mark identified with the code of the knight and the symbols associated with it suggested his ego was unconsciously prompted by the archetype of the Self to embark on a process of individuation. Jung defined individuation as follows:

> The concept of individuation plays a large role in our psychology. In general, it is the process by which individual beings are formed and differentiated; in particular, it is the development of the psychological individual (q.v.) as a being distinct from the general, collective psychology. Individuation, therefore, is a process of differentiation (q.v.), having for its goal the development of the individual personality."[38]

Two key archetypes postulated by Jung are the anima within the collective unconscious of a man and the animus within the collective unconscious of a woman. The anima and the animus are the contrasexual components within the psyche. The anima archetype symbolizes the inner feminine in every man, while the animus symbolizes the inner masculine in every woman. The anima and animus archetypes have a compensatory relationship to the persona. Jung suggests that "the anima usually contains all those qualities which the conscious attitude lacks." [39] Jung defines the function of these two archetypes as follows:

> The autonomy of the collective unconscious expresses itself in the figures of anima and animus. They personify those of its contents which, when withdrawn from projection, can be integrated into consciousness. To this extent, both figures represent functions which filter the contents of the collective unconscious through to the conscious mind.[40]

> The natural function of the animus (as well as the anima) is to remain in (their) place between individual consciousness and the collective unconscious (q.v.); exactly as the persona (q.v.) is a sort

---

[38] C.G. Jung, *Psychological Types*, p. 448.
[39] Ibid., p. 468.
[40] C.G. Jung, *Aion - Researches into the Phenomenology of the Self*, p. 20.

of stratum between the ego-consciousness and the objects of the external world. The animus and the anima should function as a bridge, or a door, leading to the images of the collective unconscious, as the persona should be a sort of bridge into the world.[41]

As there is no overt feminine image in Mark's tattoo, it stands to reason that one would ask, where does the anima manifest in this tattoo? In order to answer that question, we needed to delve into Mark's personal feeling-toned complex of shyness and insecurity. When a person is insecure, the ego is confronted on a regular basis by thoughts and feelings that undermine its sense of stability, confidence and its sense of feeling at home with itself. In Mark's case, it was the negative anima that filtered destabilizing psychological influences from the collective unconscious through to the feeling-toned complex, thus undermining the ego's self-confidence. When Mark's ego experienced the compensatory impulse from the collective unconscious (the Self), his positive anima acted to rectify this sense of insecurity by filtering the positive aspects of the Self to protect, support and heal the ego, along with the fighting spirit of the warrior to assist the ego in developing a sense of confidence. The impact of the positive anima on the ego manifested psychologically in the form of supportive and nurturing thoughts and feelings, characteristic of the positive feminine.

Our perspective holds that Jung's understanding of the psychological concept of projection is pivotal in understanding the psychology behind the tattoo. In *Mysterium Coniunctionis*, Jung writes that "all projections are unconscious identifications with the object. Every projection is simply there as an uncriticized datum of experience, and is recognized for what it is only very much later, if ever." [42] Projection, as conceptualized by Jung, is an involuntary unconscious transfer of psychological aspects of oneself onto another object or person. For example, projection shows itself in the therapeutic

---

[41] C.G. Jung, *Memories, Dreams, Reflections*, p. 392.
[42] C.G. Jung, *Mysterium Coniunctionis - An Inquiry into the Separation and Synthesis of Psychic Opposites in Alchemy.* Collected Works, Vol. 14 (Princeton: Princeton University Press, 1974) p. 488.

setting when an individual unconsciously projects aspects of their own psyche onto the therapist. This is commonly recognized as the transference. An example of a positive transference occurs when a client unconsciously transfers a positive mother or father complex onto the therapist. An instance of a negative transference is when the negative aspect of the mother or father complex is unconsciously projected onto the therapist. The transference is something that happens involuntarily to the client and, as Jung states, is simply there as an uncriticized datum of experience. While a client through his or her interaction with the therapist is consciously aware of certain components of the therapist's personality, the client is totally unaware they have projected aspects of their own personality onto the therapist. It is our experience that just as a client unconsciously transfers aspects of their psyche onto the therapist, so do people project aspects of the unconscious psyche onto the image tattooed on their skin.

It is appropriate to say something here about the physical process of imprinting a tattoo onto the skin. Although the skin constitutes the largest organ in the body, most people know little about its workings. Dr Rob Buckman, a medical doctor, professor and humorous science commentator on television, made an excellent video called "Skin - An Owner's Manual."[43] In the video, he informs his audience about the amazing qualities of their skin. Each time the heart pumps, the skin gets one-fifth of the body's blood supply. Each square inch of skin contains fifteen feet of blood vessels, which accounts for why the colour of the skin can change so rapidly. The skin is a brilliantly designed self-renewing barrier, which functions as a boundary between the inside and the outside of the body. Another interesting fact is that discarded skin cells make up ninety percent of the grey dust in one's vacuum cleaner. Approximately one billion skin cells are discarded by the human body each week, approximately the weight of a cigarette lighter. The skin is, indeed, self-renewing. The outer most protective layer of the skin is known as the epidermis. The dermis is the layer of the skin below it, which provides the elasticity

---

[43] Dr. Rob Buckman, "Skin: An Owner's Manual". Video (Detroit: Detroit Educational Television Foundation, 1999. Dr. Buckman was a medical oncologist and professor of medicine at the University of Toronto until his death in 2011.

and strength component to the skin as well as protecting it from injury.

Regarding the tattoo, it seems meaningful that the skin and the ego have similar functions to fulfill within their own domains. For the body, the skin acts as a self-renewing physiological boundary between the outer world of the environment and the inner world of the body. The ego has a similar self-renewing function between the outer world and inner worlds, but on a psychological level. The meaningful parallel between the functions of the skin and the ego merges or synchronizes with the tattoo. We see this merging or synchronization become physically concrete in the tattoo process where the tattooist imprints an image on the skin, so that psychologically the image represents the archetype that has been activated within the collective unconscious associated with the image. Therefore, the tattoo imprinted on the skin mirrors an activated archetype within the collective unconscious, which influences the ego. The ego selects an image to tattoo on the skin, without realizing that in doing so, it is being influenced by an archetype from the unconscious aligned with the image. Using one's imagination, one can readily visualize that when the image is tattooed into the skin from the outside that there is an associated image rising from the depths of the unconscious and appearing onto the skin, which we relate as analogous to the ego. In our perspective, this process is initiated with the impulse arising from the unconscious to tattoo, and experienced by the ego.

Our intuition that the tattoo is meaningfully connected to the unconscious psyche which compelled us to explore the psychology of the tattoo. Subsequent experience and acquired knowledge of the tattoo confirmed that our initial intuition was correct. Frequently, the majority of the participants in our study would speak to a sense of feeling happier upon getting a tattoo. Sometimes this positive feeling was short-lived, while sometimes it was more lasting. We believe this sense of happiness was directly related to the recipient of the tattoo unconsciously connecting to the energizing aspect of the unconscious. Von Franz spoke to the enlivening aspect that is experienced by a client entering therapy, saying "now we know that for the ego complex to get in touch with the unconscious has a vivifying and inspiring effect, and that is really the basis of all our therapeutic efforts."[44] It is our experience that participants are unconscious, for the most part, that the ego's impulse to get a tattoo originates from the depths of the collective unconscious and that the vivifying effect the ego experiences is directly related to connecting to the enlivening energies of the unconscious psyche.

Previously, we referred to Jung adopting two scientific terms, the ultraviolet and the infrared, to explain the two aspects of the archetype. We then proceeded to discuss the ultraviolet aspect of the archetypal image; the meaning associated with it. What then is the infrared aspect of the archetype with regard to the tattoo? The answer to that question is the tattoo itself. The infrared aspect of the archetype relates to the typical mode of action associated with an archetype. The typical mode of action connects the archetype to the instincts. Getting the tattoo is the action taken by the ego in response to an impulse that derives from the infrared aspect of the archetype. As we stated previously, the infrared aspect of the archetype is seamlessly and mysteriously connected, as if on a continuum, with the ultraviolet aspect of the archetypal image. It is as if the impulse from the infrared aspect of the archetype, prompting the ego to acquire a tattoo, is the unconscious trying to manifest by prompting the ego to become more conscious of the ultraviolet aspect, the psychological meaning associated with the archetypal image.

When discussing the tattoo, we can apply the expression "there's more to this than meets the eye." Mark's initial tattoo illustrates that the creation of the tattoo on the surface of the skin was simply the tip of the iceberg from a psychological perspective. Below the surface of the image, and the conscious ramifications of it, there was also a world of unseen, unconscious associations. We have utilized Mark's initial tattoo to illustrate how Jung's concepts can be of considerable assistance in understanding the multiple psychological nuances contained within a tattoo. However, there is no one-size-fits-all approach to interpreting an individual's tattoo psychologically. Each

---

[44] Marie-Louise von Franz, *On Divination and Synchronicity*, p. 20.

individual is unique, and the psychological story contained within their tattoo or tattoos cannot be obtained by overlaying an interpretative approach that is sterile, formulaic and repetitive. One needs to know the story behind each tattoo as described by the owner. Then one needs to know something about their personal life story and their understanding of their psychology and how it may connect to the tattoo. The time in their lives at which the individual obtains the tattoo is relevant, as is the area of the body where the image is tattooed. If a person has multiple tattoos, then one needs to try and understand the timing and chronology of their tattoos as they relate to their psychological story. In our experience to this point, we have seen a lot of variation among the participants, with regard to their psychological understanding of their tattoos. Many individuals saw little or no psychological meaning or relevance to their tattoos. Some saw psychological meaning in some of their tattoos, but not in others. Others insisted there was no psychological meaning contained in a particular tattoo, then seemed to contradict themselves by describing a psychological component of it. Hence, it goes without saying that one of the challenges for the interpreter is in determining the conscious and unconscious psychological components of an individual's tattoo.

Mary

"Mary" is a pseudonym.
Mary is a thirty-nine-year-old single, professional woman with a nine-year-old son. Mary left her husband several years ago as she wanted both herself and her son to be safe. According to Mary, her husband was verbally and physically abusive to her and also had drug and alcohol addictions. Mary was one of six children and the oldest of three sisters. She had two older brothers. Mary was born in Canada but her family originated from Central America. Mary described her father as having been a very authoritative presence in the household. Mary portrayed him as a strong man with a gentle side, who scared her as she was growing up. She described her father as capable of using the belt if she broke one of his implicit laws. Mary described her mother as a more boisterous personality who deferred to her husband, as that is the way within her mother's culture. Mary described both parents as passive/aggressive personalities, especially her mother. In spite of this, Mary experienced both parents as being emotionally close and supportive. She states she was closest to her two younger sisters, as they were nearer to her in age. Mary described both parents as being Christians and as being very religious. Mary did not describe herself as a Christian, but rather as religious. It was very important for her to be connected to her Mayan spiritual heritage and she made a conscious effort to integrate Mayan spirituality into her life as well as her son's.

Growing up in the family home, she experienced a power imbalance with the implicit understanding that women were supposed to defer to men. She didn't agree that the sisters should have to do chores while her brothers could go out and play. As a result of this experience, Mary indicated that she started to develop her own perspective. She experienced multiple cultural pressure points growing up in Canada. As an example, Mary recounted a time when she provided her cultural name to her teacher, spelling it for him. The teacher, however, believed Mary had misspelled her own name. The clash of her Mayan cultural heritage with Canadian culture was an ongoing issue for her. Despite the challenges she faced attending school, Mary enjoyed the learning experience. She eventually attended university, earning a degree. She really enjoyed working in her profession. She described herself as currently single with the primary focus in her life as raising her son. Mary spent most of her spare time doing various activities with her son.

Mary got her first tattoo in 2013, approximately a year after leaving her husband. It was an image of a hummingbird (see Tattoo #2 below). She had been thinking of getting this image tattooed for four years but had been unable to find a tattoo artist with the skill to create the image she wanted on her skin. According to Mary, the image was about connecting with her Mayan culture and with her people. For her, the hummingbird image signified not judging a book by its cover. Though small, Mary described the hummingbird as a warrior. The image was tattooed on her right outer thigh as she wanted it on a large surface area of the skin. Mary stated she was very happy getting the tattoo. After waiting four years to have the image tattooed on her body, she was very pleased with the result. She stated that there was nothing meaningful in the tattoo process itself for her, and that there was no psychological reason or relevance to getting the tattoo other than she thought it would make her feel happy. Mary pointed out that not many people see the tattoo, but when they do see it, they experience it more as a work of art than a tattoo, which has been a catalyst for conversation.

Tattoo 2

What was noteworthy with regard to Mary's initial tattoo was that she experienced the impulse to get a tattoo four years before actually getting it done. As previously described, the impulse to get a tattoo is experienced by the ego but does not originate there. It originates from the instinctual, unconscious foundation of the psyche. Mary knew immediately that the image she wanted tattooed on her body was that of a hummingbird, which she identified as a warrior. Therefore, in order to understand the psychology related to the hummingbird tattoo, it is important to trace its influence on Mary's ego from the original impulse to get the tattoo until the time when she got the tattoo four years later.

At the time Mary experienced the impulse to acquire a hummingbird tattoo, she was married to a man she feared. Mary stated that she felt the physical and psychological safety of both her son and herself were at risk. Therefore, it stood to reason that her ego would experience ongoing stress and anxiety related to this risk. It was within this psychological context of fear that she experienced the impulse to have an image she identified as a warrior tattooed on her skin. It was likely that the ego's stress and anxiety related to safety within the family home prompted the instinctual, unconscious foundation of Mary's psyche to send a compensatory impulse to the ego related to the warrior archetype. The ego would need a warrior's spirit to cope with the challenges posed by the domestic situation and to extricate herself and her son from this vulnerable domestic situation.

What is interesting from a psychological perspective is that even though Mary did not get the hummingbird tattoo for another four years, the psychological impact of her experiencing the impulse and making the decision to tattoo the image, which she identified as representing a warrior, suggested the ego unconsciously drew on the positive support of her instinctual, unconscious psyche to weather the difficult psychological context she was in. In her own mind, the tattoo was already present in spirit and would be actualized on the skin at the appropriate time.

Physically, Mary was small in stature. Therefore, when she used the well-known phrase "you cannot judge a book by its cover," she was also identifying with the warrior hummingbird whose physical stature was not merely small, but extremely tiny. The hummingbird tattoo on her upper right leg was actually much larger in size than an actual hummingbird. From Mary's perspective, there were no psychological connotations to the tattoo. We respectfully begged to differ. The enlargement, from an aesthetic perspective, made the artistic impression Mary wanted. However, from a psychological perspective, the enlarged image may have had something to do with Mary's ego unconsciously identifying with the warrior strength of the hummingbird and it represented an influx of compensatory positive energy. The ego unconsciously identified and aligned itself with this influx of positive instinctual energy. From a practical standpoint, the ego experienced a positive strengthening from the image and transferred this strength to the persona as it related to the domestic situation and to her outer life in general.

As noted by von Franz in her book, *The Interpretation of Fairy Tales*, from a psychological perspective birds generally symbolize "psychic entities of an intuitive and thinking character."[45] Before leaving her husband, Mary's thoughts were often characterized by anxiety and worry. Hence, the compensatory impulse to get a tattoo manifested in positive, supportive thoughts and intuitions to assist her ego in coping and to resolve her domestic situation. The positive thoughts would have manifested in ways that would support her as a woman and mother. According to Jung, the psychological function of intuition "tells you the possibilities of a situation."[46] It was likely that Mary's intuition was offering her the possibility of leaving her husband. The hummingbird image represented the activated archetype of the warrior. The activated archetype was an attempt of Mary's unconscious psyche to right the ship:

> An archetype belongs to the structure of the collective unconscious, but as the collective unconscious is in ourselves, it is also a structure of ourselves. It is part of the basic structure of our instinctual nature. Anything brought back into that instinctive pattern is supposed to be cured. This structure of man is supposed to be a wholly adapted animal, a remarkable thing able to live perfectly. Most of our psychogenic ills consist in the fact that we have deviated from the instinctive pattern of man. We suddenly find ourselves in the air, our tree no longer receives the nourishing substance from the earth. So you see, when you get back into an archetypal situation you are in your right instinctive attitude in which you must be when you want to live on the earth's surface; in your right atmosphere with your right food, etc. The archetype is the instinctive natural man, as he has always been. The old priests and medicine men understood this, not by knowledge, but by intuition.[47]

Anxieties and worries are feeling-toned complexes from the personal unconscious influencing the ego in a negative and destabilizing way. The compensatory contents of the archetype of the warrior that brought support, empowerment and protection were filtered to the ego via the positive aspect of Mary's animus.

---

[45] Marie-Louise von Franz, *The Interpretation of Fairy Tales* (Dallas: Spring Publications, 1987) p. 48.
[46] C.G. Jung, *Dream Analysis: Notes on the Seminar Given in 1928-30*, p. 315.
[47] Ibid., p. 129.

A woman's animus is the contrasexual archetype operating within the collective unconscious whose function psychologically is to filter contents from the collective unconscious to the ego. Interestingly, the *Penguin Dictionary of Symbols* has the following to say about the hummingbird:

> The Hopi Indians of Arizona, who are related at least linguistically to the Aztecs, have a myth in which the hummingbird intercedes with the god of germination and plant growth to save mankind from famine. (Leo W. Simmons in Tals pp. 431-2) The same positive valency determines the view of the Colombian Tukano Indians that the hummingbird, or fly-bird, has sexual intercourse with flowers and stands for glowing virility as the erect male phallus.[48]

Mary got the tattoo of the hummingbird a year after leaving her husband. The tattoo exuded freedom, colour, a warrior's spirit and a celebratory sense of release. It was as if the tattoo reflected the sense of release Mary experienced upon leaving the man who, according to Mary, compromised the safety and wellbeing of both her and her son. Also, Mary's initial and subsequent tattoos reflected characteristics and personal storylines related to Mary that she now felt safe to express.

As discussed previously, Jung defines archetypes as forms of instinct. The warrior archetype and the animus are two such instinctual forms operating within the collective unconscious. However, as previously stated, it is an aspect of Jung's hypothesis that the central regulating centre of all the archetypes of the collective unconscious is the Self. Therefore, when the impulse of the warrior archetype was constellated in Mary's psyche, and the archetype of her animus was functioning and filtering contents of the collective unconscious to her ego, the impulse of the warrior archetype and the animus were being set in motion and regulated by the archetype of the Self.

---

[48] Jean Chevalier and Alain Gheerbrant, *The Penguin Dictionary of Symbols* (London: Penguin Books, 1996) p. 531.

In addition to representing thoughts and intuition, birds may also refer to the soul.[49] Speaking to the soul reference, Robin Lea Hutton wrote in her contribution to a book honouring the memory of Marie-Louise von Franz (*The Fountain of the Love of Wisdom*), an article in which she shares synchronistic experiences related to birds and a meaningful coincidence:

> As I write this, I remember a story von Franz told of either an analysand or a famous person she knew who had a bird try for the longest time to get into this person's home by flying into a closed window. No matter where the person went, the bird followed, always flying into a closed window. The person totally ignored the bird, even tried to shoo it away if I remember correctly. Von Franz said that the bird was the man's soul trying to get in, because like all of us, he had gotten so caught up in the existential world of ego goals and pursuit of power and success that he was totally ignoring his whole inner life, his soul. The bird was desperately trying to come in and call attention to the fact that he has to divert some attention back and take care of the soul. Unfortunately the man just saw the bird as a pest, so he ignored it and went off and had some sort of catastrophe. Oh, dear.[50]

Interestingly, given Mary's tattoo, Hutton shares a personal story in which, a few months before writing the article, she caught a hummingbird that had become trapped inside her house and was trying to find a way to get back outside. She realized through this synchronistic event that the Self was trying to get her attention about something.[51] Jung conceptualized such synchronistic events as creative moments in time wherein psyche and matter come together in a meaningful way.[52]

In the early 1970s, a television series titled "Kung Fu" starring David Carradine became popular. In that show, David Carradine played Kwai Chang Caine, nicknamed "Grasshopper" during his

---

[49] Marie-Louise von Franz, *The Interpretation of Fairy Tales*, p. 48.
[50] Emmanuel Kennedy-Xypolitas (ed.), *The Fountain of the Love of Wisdom* (Wilmette, Illinois: Chiron Publications, 2006) pp. 273-274.
[51] Ibid., p. 273.
[52] Marie-Louise von Franz, *On Divination and Synchronicity*, p. 54.

apprenticeship. During one of the early episodes where "Grasshopper" was undergoing his training with a Shaolin monk, he was told that "when the soul is in danger, the soul must become a warrior."[53] This phrase resonates with what we observed in Mary's attempts to empower herself in a situation where she was threatened with both loss of physical safety and loss of soul. It was likely that Mary suffered a loss of soul in her difficult marriage and that the impulse from the collective unconscious was an instinctual response for her to reclaim her soul through the spirit of the warrior. Ultimately, that impulse originated and was regulated by the Self, as explained earlier. In *Psychological Types*, Jung differentiates between what he means by the terms "psyche" and "soul"; "by the psyche I understand the totality of all psychic processes, conscious and unconscious. By soul, on the other hand, I understand a clearly demarcated functional complex that can best be described as a 'personality'."[54] An example of a psychic process related to Mary's tattoo is that empowering thoughts and feelings were transmitted from Mary's positive animus to the ego. An example of the soul returning is when the ego renews itself by creating a persona that is suffused with a personality of strength, determination and resilience. Eventually, Jung came to the realization that there is a compensatory relationship between the persona and the anima/animus.[55] Jung describes the anima/animus as the soul-image. Below he explains the anima as soul-image in a man (in a woman he describes the animus as soul-image):

> The soul-image is a specific image (q.v.) among those produced by the unconscious. Just as the persona (v. Soul), or outer attitude, is represented in dreams by images of definite persons who possess the outstanding qualities of the persona in especially marked form, so in a man the soul i.e., anima, or inner attitude, is represented in the unconscious by definite persons with the corresponding qualities. Such an image is called a 'soul-image'.[56]

---

[53] *Kung Fu* (1972 TV series) from *Wikipedia,* the free encyclopedia.
[54] C.G. Jung, *Psychological Types*, p. 463.
[55] C.G. Jung, *Dream Analysis: notes on the Seminar given in 1928-30,* p. 52.
[56] C.G. Jung, *Psychological Types*, p. 470.

It was possible Mary's persona, as a result of a difficult and compromising marriage, became weakened, worn down, and experienced a loss of soul. The compensating image of the warrior's spirit to the ego made possible a strengthening of the persona, of a return of soul. Her sense of happiness was reflected in the vibrant, colourful hummingbird. It was as if her soul had been liberated.

Mary's next tattoo came approximately three years after the hummingbird tattoo, in 2016. She was visiting the country of her parents' birth with her entire family. The immersion in an environment where Mayan cultural and religious heritage still played a prominent role was meaningful for her. She wanted to get a tattoo that deepened her connection to her cultural and religious lineage and also reflected the emotional bond between herself and her son. To accomplish this, she selected an image representing the birth sign for each of them from a specific Mayan calendar (see Tattoo #3 below). The images were tattooed on her sternum area. Mary chose the area situated close to her heart and to the area of her body where she carried her son during pregnancy. Again, Mary stated there was no noticeable impact on her psychological attitude other than experiencing a sense of happiness upon getting the tattoo.

Although it was some four years since leaving her husband, her second tattoo reflected her ongoing dedication to the warrior spirit of defending what matters most to her, the life of her son, her own life and the quality of the life she envisioned for them both. The impulse that led to the hummingbird tattoo constellated her warrior's spirit to defend their safety and well-being. Three years after that initial tattoo, she tattooed the Mayan birth sign for each of them. As it was centrally located on the front of her body, the tattoo suggests that Mary's intention remained focused on her life and that of her son and her desire that each of them be meaningfully connected to her Mayan heritage.

Before unpacking the various psychological associations of the second tattoo, it is important to talk about the origin of the birth signs. The birth signs derive from the Tzolkin Mayan calendar. The calendar is based on a 260-day cycle developed from astronomical observations and shamanic trance states. The calendar is designed according to a mathematical and spiritual understanding of meaning ascribed to numbers. Mary's son's sign is called *Ajaw*, the light. The tattoo had the son's birth sign situated above Mary's birth sign. Directly below the son's sign were four dots with a horizontal line underneath. In this culture, each dot represents one while a straight line symbolizes the number five. Hence, the four single dots plus the line underneath represent the number nine. Mary's sign was known as *Ix* or *Hix*, the jaguar. Again, the four dots under her sign represented the number four.[57] The background of the second tattoo artistically contains a mixture of the colours red, blue, purple, turquoise, and green.

Tattoo 3

The impulse for the second tattoo emanated from the positive mother archetype which ultimately is associated with the Self. It was readily apparent from the images and the area they were placed that Mary's ego was directing its focus towards her son. This was evident in her conversation with us in the data collecting phase of the study, as she repeatedly emphasized that her son was her primary focus in life.

---

[57] Maya Calendar. (2024, August 8). In *Wikipedia*. en.wikipedia.org/wiki/Maya_calendar

Therefore, Mary's tattoo on the level of the persona reflected that she identified with her role as a loving, caring mother. Although the visibility of this second tattoo was dependent on what she was wearing, at all times Mary knew the tattoo was there. She told the interviewer that the psychological connotations of this tattoo were to strengthen the emotional bond between her and her son as well as to connect her to her cultural and religious heritage. Hence, the tattoo acted as an ongoing psychological catalyst to aid and abet the ego and its creation, the persona, as it attempted to embody the psychological goals she identified with and projected upon this second tattoo.

The Tzolkin calendar (known as the Maya Sacred Round or 260-day calendar) is, as the name implies, a circle. Situated within the sacred circle is a smaller inner circle consisting of 20 named days, two of which are Mary and her son's birth signs. Each birth sign is composed of an oval-shaped head encompassed by a square with rounded corners. The larger Maya Sacred Round is in the shape of a mandala and the two birth signs similarly have mandala connotations. As mentioned earlier, the mandala represents the regulatory, ordering and regenerative aspect of the psyche. It symbolizes wholeness and the coming together of both the conscious and unconscious aspects of the psyche. Mandalas generally appear psychologically at a time when an individual is experiencing a sense of disorientation, confusion and chaos. As stated in the previous chapter, the essential characteristic of the mandala is that it points to orientation in chaos, by bringing order and meaning.

Although at the time of the second tattoo it had been approximately four years since Mary had left her troubled marriage, there was by necessity a time of psychological transition as she attempted to forge a better life for herself and her son. The first tattoo of the warrior hummingbird, acquired a year after leaving the husband, conveyed a sense of liberation and return of spirit and soul. Nonetheless, the ongoing reality in the aftermath of leaving the husband and father of her child was a time of psychological disorientation, confusion and chaos. Hence, Mary's ego experienced an impulse from the Self, to compensate the sense of inner disorder of the ego with the ordering mandala birth sign images found in the Maya Sacred Round calendar.

The Maya Sacred Round calendar is based on numbers. From the quantitative perspective, this calendar based on numbers allows the Mayans to count and measure time. However, from a qualitative perspective, the numbers aspect of the calendar symbolizes the ordering aspect that underlies the archetypes. Jung defines the psychological aspect of numbers as the archetype of "order made conscious." That the Mayan Sacred Round calendar is a circle and a mandala, symbolizes the ordering factor of the central archetype of the collective unconscious, the Self. Mary would not be conscious of the fact that by selecting and identifying with the Maya Sacred Round calendar and the birth signs related to herself and her son, she was accessing a numerical ordering factor that underlies the archetype of the Self. The mandala is also associated with the number four. One of the symbolic connotations of the number four is that it represents the archetypal potential for wholeness of the individual personality. The Mayan calendar itself is based on the meaningful significance of numbers. Therefore, it is quite interesting that Mary gravitated to this source for her second tattoo. Beyond the association of the number four related to the mandala images of the two birth signs, were four dots under each birth sign. As the reader can see, the symbolic significance of the number four resonated throughout the tattoo images.

There is one other number to be discussed in relationship to the birth signs: namely, the number two. Mary wanted to strengthen the emotional bond between herself and her son by tattooing both their birth signs on her sternum. From a strictly quantitative perspective, she is one person while her son is another, so one plus one equals two. This clearly reflected the reality of their situation, and part of the persona/ego aspect of the number two that was reflected in Mary's tattoo. However, as discussed in the opening chapter, Jung was powerfully influenced by the Chinese approach to numbers, which emphasized their qualitative or archetypal aspect. Jung emphasized that the number two possesses an important relationship to what he called the threshold phenomena of consciousness. This means that the number two surfaces when a content of the unconscious is approaching the threshold of consciousness as "a recognizable entity, taking the first step, as it were, toward manifestation."[58] From this perspective, what was it in Mary that was approaching the ego from the unconscious? The number two, from the qualitative perspective, symbolizes the coming to consciousness of the animus, the contrasexual archetype within Mary's unconscious whose function is to filter contents from the collective unconscious to the ego. We view the birth sign tattoo as representing not only the chronological birth dates of Mary and her son, but also the unconscious manifestation of her positive animus projected onto her son's birth sign. When Mary linked her birth sign to that of her son, and included the two signs in the same tattoo, it symbolized from a depth psychology perspective that the ultraviolet meaning or content related to the contrasexual archetype, the animus, attempted to cross the threshold from the collective unconscious into her ego consciousness. In Mary's case, it was specifically the positive aspect of her animus that was constellated and seeking conscious recognition.

Mary was not aware of the psychological connotation of the numerical archetypes that underlie her second tattoo. However, the impulse to acquire a tattoo derived from the Maya Sacred Round, a calendar based on the ordering, spiritual and meaningful aspects of numbers, suggests that Mary instinctually gravitated to such an archetype within the collective unconscious. As such, the numerical connotations of the tattoo, like her positive animus, were also wanting to cross the threshold of the unconscious into consciousness.

Mary asserted that she wanted to deepen her and her son's emotional connection to her Mayan cultural and religious heritage. This would constitute the aspect of the mandala that has to do with deriving meaning out of chaos and confusion. Jung wrote "only gradually did I discover what the mandala really is: 'Formation, Transformation, Eternal Mind's eternal recreation.' And that is the self, the wholeness of the personality, which if all goes well is harmonious, but which

---

[58] Marie-Louise von Franz, *Number and Time*, p. 92.

cannot tolerate self-deceptions."[59] It was obvious upon meeting Mary and listening to her story that she was a woman of determination and integrity. Her decision to search for a meaningful alternative to her difficult domestic situation with integrity resulted in an impulse from the Self which led her to a mandala image from her own heritage, the Maya Sacred Round calendar. This powerful image resonated with a bedrock of ancient meaning for Mary to anchor her life upon and draw ongoing sustenance for her heart, soul and mind. It is our contention that the psychological dynamics associated with the mandala, a symbolic representation of the Self, were unconsciously projected by her ego onto the tattoo.

Behind the birth sign tattoos is a dynamic splash of colour. The colour backdrop contained a shifting amalgam of predominantly violet and red hues. The colours suggested the depth of emotion associated with the tattoos and the vivifying and inspiring effect the impulse for the tattoo has upon the ego. This positive emotional effect, which Mary characterized as happiness, was part of the impact of the impulse for the tattoo that was experienced by her ego and transmitted to the persona.

Mary's third and most recent tattoo came two years after the birth signs, in 2018. This third tattoo was placed on her inner right wrist, as she wanted it to be visible. This image was of three worry dolls (see Tattoo #4 below). Worry dolls are small dolls handmade using wire and colourful textile products. The dolls relate to a Mayan legend in which a princess, named Ixmucane, receives from her father the sun god the gift of having the capacity to solve any problem a human could face. In the Mayan tradition, worry dolls are given to children with worries and troubles. The children place the worry dolls under their pillows before going to bed. It is believed they will wake the next morning to find all their worries are gone.[60] Mary said she got this tattoo to further connect her to her sisters and to her Mayan cultural heritage. Her sisters each got similar tattoos. She described feeling more connected to her sisters and the Mayan

---

[59] C.G. Jung, *Memories, Dreams, Reflections*, ed. Aniela Jaffe, pp. 195-196.
[60] Worry Doll. (2024, October 1). In *Wikipedia*. en.wikipedia.org/wiki/Worry_doll

culture as a result of the tattoo. She indicated that she associated no other psychological connotation with the tattoo.

Tattoo 4

The third tattoo, like the previous two tattoos, was beautiful in its artistic design and use of colour. In discussing the third tattoo with the interviewer, Mary related the Mayan story about the worry dolls and their role of relieving a child of troublesome thoughts and worries. However, she made no connection to an idea that she acquired the tattoo to assist either her son or herself with worries. Rather, Mary emphasized the emotional connection to her sisters and to her Mayan heritage. While not discounting Mary's comments about her own tattoo, we hypothesized that there were possibly psychological implications in the tattoo about which Mary was unconscious.

It is important to look at the conscious components of the tattoo. Mary had two sisters. Therefore, the three worry dolls represent Mary and her two sisters. She did not indicate which of the dolls represented herself. The three dolls from the perspective of Mary's ego were images representing the three sisters. That the dolls also represented the Mayan culture completed Mary's intention of having the worry dolls deepen the emotional connection between her and her sisters and her Mayan heritage. The fact that the tattoo was visible to her on her inner right wrist allowed her ego to visually reinforce this connection on an ongoing basis. The visibility aspect of the tattoo also assisted her persona to share with the outside world a part of herself with which she was currently identified. The reference to her sisters and her Mayan heritage was something that would not be immediately apparent to others. However, the specific references related to the tattoo were readily shared by Mary when asked by an interested observer.

From our perspective, the full import of the third tattoo can only be realized by considering its place as the third in a sequence of tattoos. The impulse of the first tattoo experienced by the ego activates the warrior archetype within the collective unconscious. The warrior's spirit, its support and strength, were qualities and contents filtered to the ego via the positive animus. This warrior's spirit allowed Mary's ego to defend the safety and wellbeing of herself and her son and to divorce her husband. The primary focus of Mary's life was to ensure that her son experience a safe and loving environment. As such, the role Mary instinctively identified with was that of mother. Hence, simultaneous to the activation of the warrior archetype was the activation of the positive aspect of the mother archetype within the collective unconscious. The warrior archetype allows the ego to operationalize and constellate the positive aspects of the mother. Once again in Mary's case, the positive aspects of the mother archetype were filtered to the ego via the positive animus.

Subsequent to her first tattoo was the impulse experienced by the ego that lead to the second tattoo, the image of the mother and son birth signs. Once again, with the second tattoo, it was possible to see the degree to which Mary identified with the positive aspects of the mother archetype. The spirit of the warrior archetype constellated in her first tattoo continued to function and assist the ego in the second tattoo.

The worry dolls tattoo followed the second tattoo. When discussing the third tattoo, Mary made no reference to qualities related to motherhood. Nonetheless, it is our viewpoint that the impulse experienced by the ego in the third tattoo originated from the positive aspects of a feminine archetype within the collective unconscious. This positive feminine archetype is ultimately connected to the mother archetype and the Self. We speculate that Mary's omission of references to motherhood with regard to the worry dolls tattoo was because she was unconscious of this reference.

In relating her personal, psychological story, Mary did not characterize herself as a person who worried a lot. However, as we observed her situation, worrying was an ongoing aspect of her psychology. Mary's mental status during her difficult marriage, when she was constantly concerned about her and her son's safety, was a time when it is reasonable to assume anxieties and worries would have been prevalent within her mind. The first impulse from the unconscious, the second impulse and then the third impulse to get a tattoo can be viewed from standpoint as attempts by the unconscious to compensate for and alleviate Mary's worries about herself, her son, and life in general.

It is a parent and usually the mother that gives the worry doll to a child. By identifying with the Mayan legend regarding the worry doll, Mary was identifying with the mother's capacity to alleviate her son's worries and troubles. However, regarding Mary's own psychology, the impulse to tattoo the worry doll symbolized an impulse from her unconscious to connect her to the positive feminine aspects of her psyche, so that she not only alleviated the worries related to her son, but also redirected some of those positive dynamics towards herself. By having identified with a symbol of the positive feminine and the mother, Mary was identifying with that aspect of herself that could tend to her own inner child. The child symbolizes potential, possibilities and life yet to be lived. This ultimately has to do with Mary developing the full range of her potential as a woman. That her tattoos have such a beautiful, artistic quality suggested Mary had creative aspects of herself that were yet to be lived.

Princess Ixmucane is given the gift of dispelling worries and troubles by her father, the sun god. The mother and father archetypes constitute masculine and feminine regulatory components of the

Self. Hence, the princess, by connection to the mother archetype, is accessing a regulatory aspect of the Self. Psychological wholeness is approximated when masculine and feminine archetypes within the collective unconscious align in a way that supports and underlies the conscious life of an individual. The Mayan legend of the worry doll reflects this archetypal blueprint for potential psychological wholeness. The princess, the feminine, connects to the positive mother archetype through the positive father archetype, the sun god. The sun god symbolizes the positive archetypal logos that, when activated and transmitted to the ego, allows it to think in ways that dispel worries and troubles. As the mother and father archetypes are aligned in this legend, this symbolizes that the logos contents of the father archetype are aligned with the eros aspect of the mother archetype. This manifests and supports the activation of positive thought processes with a nurturing love, a mother's love. Practically, this means that feelings of love and positive nurturance underlie and accompany a positive, life-enhancing thought process.

Mary related in her personal history that one of the salient factors that influenced her psychological development was the power imbalance in the family where women were supposed to defer to men. She did not agree that the sisters should have had to do chores while her brothers were free to go out and play. As a result, Mary began to develop her own perspective. It is noteworthy that Jung describes the qualitative aspect of the number three as representing dynamic movement which allows the ultimate unity represented by the number one to become recognizable in time.[61] The three tattoos can be viewed as steps along the way towards Mary finding and strengthening her feminine voice. In discussing the symbolic import of the number three and its connotations with regard to processes being realized in time, there appeared to be a concordance between Mary developing her feminine voice and the number three, towards new positive developments being realized in her life.

Here we have outlined our understanding of the psychological storyline associated with Mary's tattoos. Mary was aware of some of

---

[61] Marie-Louise von Franz, *Number and Time*, pp. 102-103

the elements of this psychological story, but not all of them. An aspect of our original hypothesis, as explained in the introduction, is that the impulse to get a tattoo experienced by Mary derived from the archetypal foundation of the psyche, the collective unconscious. With the passage of time, the possibility exists for the ego to become more conscious of the psychological meaning associated with the archetypal image, the ultraviolet aspect of the archetype. Each of her tattoos represented the infrared aspect of the archetype, the mode of action taken by the ego in response to the impulse from the collective unconscious. Mary's ego was unaware that it had projected the ultraviolet aspect of the archetype onto the skin via the tattoo.

Mary planned on acquiring another tattoo approximately a year from the date of our interview for this project. She planned on getting either an image of mother earth, a bird woman or a water woman. She indicated the tattoo was intended to assist herself and her son to strengthen their connection to the Mayan culture. The plan was for her fourth tattoo to be a big piece on the upper part of either her right or left arm. Again, the fourth impulse from the unconscious to her ego for a tattoo was related to strengthening her bond to her son and her heritage. It was apparent that the positive aspect of the mother archetype from the collective unconscious continued to influence Mary. She, for the most part, appeared unconscious of the mother connotations of the tattoo. Whatever image of a woman Mary ultimately selected for her fourth tattoo, it is obvious that the development and support of her feminine voice is a major component.

Joseph

"Joseph" is a pseudonym. At the time of his participation, Joseph was thirty-three years old. Raised in what he described as a lower middle-class family, his parents divorced when he was sixteen. He has two brothers. The father was portrayed as being a racist, homophobic, macho type of man with false masculine pride. Joseph described him as stubborn and manipulative. In addition, the father displayed a lack of respect for Joseph and his friends. Joseph said he and his father have not spoken to one another in years as they have nothing to talk about. Joseph spoke of his close relationship to his mother. He described her as an unhappy woman who worked fulltime while trying to raise the boys. He said she had a difficult time doing so. She had not finished high school. Although Joseph described her as very anxious, prone to worrying about everything, with a tendency towards impatience, he said he felt loved by his mother. Joseph believed his mother trusted him more than the other boys. The family moved constantly, never staying in one location longer than two years. The last family home was lost to bankruptcy.

Joseph shared a room with his two brothers when growing up. His brothers participated in sports, while Joseph pursued activities in the arts. He stated that his parents were religious when the boys were young, but he described himself as a confirmed atheist, saying the Bible contained too many contradictions. He said his parents did not have mental health or substance abuse issues. He did not want to end up closed-minded like his dad. He believed his father must have hated the fact that Joseph is gay. Joseph believed his unstable family environment contributed to a chronic sense of insecurity, and that he was constantly afraid of everything. He did not enjoy primary school due to his fears. However, he enjoyed theatre school. He'd come to the realization that his anxiety was a disorder only in recent years. He was not on any medication at the time of the interview and did not drink alcohol or take street drugs. Not studious by nature, he described himself as a fast learner with leadership skills. Joseph aspired to being a sensitive, flexible and open-minded person. He worked hard, balancing two jobs while training for a future profession. He did not have much free time, but when he did, he played video games, spent time with his friends and allocated time to self-care. At the time of the interview, Joseph was in a romantic relationship that he described as going well. He was satisfied with his life and looked forward to the future, believing life held much more for him.

Joseph experienced his first impulse to acquire a tattoo when he was seventeen. The tattoo depicted a clown on the upper right portion of his back. While working at summer camp, he had seen an image of a clown that he liked very much drawn by a female camp co-worker. At the same time, he had been learning about the art of clowning in acting class. He selected the back placement as he was not committed, at that point, to having a tattoo on a more visible area. Later, when he was more committed, he placed tattoos on areas of the body that could be seen by others.

The initial tattoo process was meaningful for Joseph. He felt he had gone through an initiation. He traces this to the fact that he had committed himself to the blood and the pain of the process and that he had something lasting to show for it when it was over. He suggested there may have been some psychological component to his first tattoo. As Joseph said he was a very scared teenager, he believed getting the tattoo opened him up to other possibilities. It was an affirmative moment where he said -- yes, I can do this. The fact that he was allowed to acquire a tattoo at such a young age felt like an initiation into something that he planned on repeating.

The clown tattoo was no longer visible on Joseph's back as he covered it up five years later with his second tattoo. The clown in the theatre and carnival world is a figure usually associated with laughter and comic relief. However, some clowns have sad eyes and behaviour which suggests there is more to the clown than merely being a catalyst for laughter. The clown, historically, is associated with the trickster figure. Jung relates various symbolic aspects of the trickster:

He is a forerunner of the saviour, and, like him, God, man, and animal at once. He is both subhuman and superhuman, a bestial and divine being, whose chief and most alarming characteristic is his unconsciousness. Because of it he is deserted by his (evidently human) companions, which seems to indicate that he has fallen below their level of consciousness. He is so unconscious of himself that his body is not a unity, and his two hands fight each other... From his penis he makes all kinds of useful plants. This is a reference to his original nature as a creator, for the world is made from the body of a god. On the other hand he is in many respects stupider than the animals, and gets into one ridiculous scrape after another. Although he is not really evil, he does the most atrocious things from sheer unconsciousness and unrelatedness.[62]

Also, the clown/trickster generally symbolizes a reversal of order; for example, the jester at a royal court playfully undermines the status of the king and royal court authority. The clown/trickster represents irreverence, the ridiculous, the mocking of authority.[63]

Joseph was an adolescent when he acquired his first tattoo. From a psychological perspective, adolescence is a time when the ego is quite labile. Transitioning from childhood to adulthood, the adolescent ego experiences the thousand and one possibilities of life, without yet having the wisdom and psychological wherewithal that comes with experience. Hence, the adolescent ego's conscious stability, mood and orientation often fluctuate dramatically as it attempts to navigate life's challenges. For Joseph, adolescence was a time fraught with chronic insecurities, anxiety and fear. Despite the love he experienced from his mother, her own deep-seated anxieties and constant worrying contributed to his own chronic anxieties. Joseph's lack of respect for what he described as his father's closed-minded attitudes, false pride and narrow definition of masculinity, led him to identify with the rebel. Therefore, he developed an ongoing resistance to authority and mainstream values and

---

[62] C.G. Jung, *The Archetypes and the Collective Unconscious*, Collected Works, Vol. 9, Part 1 (Princeton University Press, 1975) pp. 263-264.
[63] Jean Chevalier and Alain Gheerbrant, *The Penguin Dictionary of Symbols*, p. 207.

perspectives. In the midst of all this, Joseph's artistic temperament and creativity were burgeoning.

The impulse that led to the clown tattoo was a threshold moment for Joseph in that a new world of possibilities opened up for him. According to Joseph, crossing this threshold was the psychological significance of the clown tattoo. It was the aesthetic and not the psychological aspect, however, that figured most prominently in Joseph's decision-making when selecting and designing the image to be tattooed on his skin. The clown represented an aesthetic and artistic persona with which he identified. It also represented the rebel aspect of his persona, of being outside the mainstream, of being a gay man, and of saying yes to all that. It's unclear if Joseph was aware that the clown is associated with the trickster figure. It is possible he was conscious of this association, at least to some degree, as he was teaching an arts class on the topic of clowning at the time.

It is noteworthy that one of the salient characteristics of the trickster is unconsciousness. Psychological unconsciousness is fairly typical for an adolescent, whose left hand does not know what the right hand is doing most of the time. Nonetheless, the unconscious aspect related to the trickster is evident in Joseph's belief that his tattoos hold primarily aesthetic rather than psychological significance for him. Unbeknownst to Joseph, his identification with the trickster archetype produced an element of psychological unconsciousness within the attitude of the ego. In keeping with the preceding statement, it should not be surprising then that when Joseph identified with the clown/trickster image, he was unconscious of the multitude of psychological connotations related to it.

The first impulse to get a tattoo is highly significant. It is somewhat similar to a person's recollection of their first important dream, wherein a psychological blueprint is laid out in symbolic language. Hence, it is important to know that the trickster archetype, associated with the alchemical Mercurius, is but one of Mercurius' multiple aspects. Another aspect of Mercurius is that he symbolizes the Self and the process of individuation.[64] We believe that the impulse experienced by Joseph at the age of seventeen can be traced back to the Self. The salient features of the initial tattoo are the aesthetic connotation, the theme of the rebel, of being outside the mainstream and the unconsciousness associated with the archetype of the trickster.

The second impulse to get a tattoo occurred in Joseph's twentieth year. He wanted an image of Hermes. However, he delayed acquiring the Hermes tattoo for five years until he located a tattooist he trusted to do the artistic rendering he wanted. During the five-year wait for the Hermes tattoo, he acquired other tattoos. Nonetheless, we will follow the chronological sequence of Joseph's *impulses* to tattoo as it best reflects his psychological process. When discussing his reasons for wanting Hermes tattooed on his right arm, Joseph related that Hermes is the god of fire, art and intelligence. He indicated that he was involved in theatre and the arts and that the creative qualities of Hermes resonated with him. What Joseph omitted in his associations around the image is that Hermes is known as "the divine trickster" and protector of thieves. Psychologically, this suggested that the unconsciousness associated with the trickster archetype, which is related to the clown image, continued with the impulse to tattoo the Hermes image. Also, with the second impulse, the aspect of the rebel, the transgressor and confronter of mainstream norms associated with the trickster archetype continued to influence the ego. On multiple occasions throughout his Collected Works, Jung comments that Hermes is a synonym for Mercurius.[65]

With the second impulse, a psychological transition has evidently taken place. With the clown tattoo, the adolescent ego's persona aligned itself with a clown's demeanor and perspective. Joseph indicated that he selected the image primarily for aesthetic reasons. At the same time, the image was something an adolescent would choose to flout authority while being unconscious of its deeper psychological ramifications. With the passing of three years and

---

[64] C.G. Jung, *Alchemical Studies*. Collected Works, Vol. 13 (Princeton: Princeton University Press, 1970) p. 237.
[65] Ibid., pp. 202-3.

leaving adolescence behind, the ego identified with Hermes, an image that for now twenty-year-old Joseph was representative of intellectual and creative prowess. The idea that the Self is the origin of his impulses to tattoo crystallizes with the third impulse, and second tattoo: a flower mandala imprinted on his back (see Tattoo #5 below).

Tattoo 5

Joseph claimed the mandala image did not represent anything to him. He stated that he held the image for two months, consulting with two different tattooists before getting the mandala tattooed on his upper right back. He said he wanted a bigger image and liked the size of the flower mandala design. According to Joseph, the main reason for selecting the back as location was to cover the initial clown tattoo. What is noteworthy is that while claiming the mandala image held no meaning for him, he said there was more psychological relevance to this tattoo than any of his others. He declared that he felt more adult and ready for the future after this tattoo. He said he felt different with this second tattoo on his body and liked how he felt. He was excited to have a major piece of body art on him and was excited to show it to everyone. He mentioned this tattoo solidified his commitment to acquiring further tattoos. He stated he felt more of a rebel afterwards, and was more committed to selecting future designs and colours that represented him more fully after the flower mandala tattoo. He wanted to show others that one could acquire tattoos, be different, and still be a good person. A stigma has often been associated with the tattoo throughout Europe and North America whether or not the tattoo is in fashion. The stigma has to do with questionable morality and character.

As noted in the previous chapter, the image of a mandala often manifests when an individual is experiencing a period of psychological crisis, confusion or disorientation. Joseph described himself as having an undiagnosed anxiety disorder at that time. As such, he was persistently challenged by fears and insecurities. This ongoing sense of insecurity resulted in Joseph experiencing a compensatory impulse from the Self to assuage and stabilize the ego. The flower is a well-known symbol of the Self. In our understanding, the unfolding symmetry of the flower symbolizes the unfolding of psychological life from its centre in the collective unconscious.

Joseph's act to cover the clown tattoo, saying it no longer represented him, does not mean the trickster archetype's influence on the ego was diminished. That the trickster's influence continued was evident in Joseph's impulse to get the Hermes tattoo. The unconsciousness associated with the trickster can be seen to manifest in Joseph's statement that the mandala image did not represent anything to him. Meanwhile, it was the ego's identification with the mandala image that brought order and protection to it. The right hand not knowing what the left hand was doing reflected the unconsciousness associated with the trickster. Joseph, despite saying the mandala tattoo held more psychological relevance than any of the other tattoos, was unconscious of the fact that it was the symmetrical, ordering aspect of the mandala which assisted the ego in experiencing a transition to a psychological state of adulthood and to feeling more grounded and hopeful about the future.

Each of the first three impulses to get a tattoo originated from the Self. However, there was a marked difference between the impulse from the trickster aspect of the Self and the ordering mandala aspect of the Self. The trickster manifested psychologically more as an interplay of opposites within the ego. How the ego responds to that interplay determines its impact on the individual's life. The trickster, while containing the possibility for psychological growth and development, did not bring the protective, healing and calming influence to the ego which the mandala aspect of the Self did. It was significant that, from this point forward, Joseph's tattoos frequently contained mandala images.

Joseph acquired his next tattoo at the age of twenty-four. He and a female friend decided to get matching tattoos of a key (see Tattoo #6 below). He placed it on his left arm as he wanted it to be readily visible. Initially, he did not like the image standing on its own. Once the image of the key was surrounded by other tattoos, however, he grew to accept and like it. For Joseph, the key represented the capacity to unlock future possibilities. He indicated that, from this point onward, his tattoos were selected for aesthetic reasons and not for the meaning behind them. Again, it is our understanding that Joseph's unconsciousness regarding the meaning behind his tattoo images was an ongoing effect of the trickster archetype on his attitude.

Tattoo 6

The key symbolizes the capacity to lock or unlock something, be it a room, the meaning hidden in our memories or a situation in life. *The Book of Symbols* has the following to say about the key:

> Keys evoke the tension between seeking and finding, restricting and releasing, withholding and giving, prohibiting and admitting. The individual and the "key" momentarily becomes threshold guardian and opener of the way. Human consciousness perpetually searches for the key that will give it access to the object of its longing—self-discovery, peace of mind, the enigmatic heart of the beloved. The difference between being shut out and getting in seems as tantalizingly simple as an antique key sliding into a keyhole.[66]

The impulse for the key tattoo followed the flower mandala. As mentioned, the key represents the capacity to unlock future possibilities. The key image was like a symbolic signpost for Joseph regarding the tattoo in general. Again, his primary reason for the tattoo related to aesthetics. This meant that he liked the way it looked and how it felt on his body, despite the fact that it took a period of time for him to appreciate it.

The key image contained a mandala component of four interconnected elements in the shape of a cross centred within a square at the top of the key. Again, the square and the cross are both connected to the number four, which is the qualitative numerical ordering factor underlying the psychological potential for wholeness. It was as if Joseph, at some unconscious level, experienced the ordering and centreing aspect of the image. He was completely unconscious of the fact that the mandala image originated from the Self, which was responding to his ongoing fears and insecurities. It was as if Joseph had unconsciously discovered a way forward, a key to assuaging the fears and anxieties of his ego by incorporating the mandala image into his tattoos. The projection of the mandala onto the skin allowed the ego to unconsciously anchor itself with the Self.

---

[66] Ami Ronnenberg and Kathleen Martin, editors, *The Book of Symbols – Reflections on Archetypal Images* (Cologne, Germany: Taschen, 2010) p. 562.

Joseph's next impulse to tattoo occurred in the same year. He was doing contract work at the time and was directed by a superior to terminate an employee who had a tattoo that conflicted with the public image the company was trying to project. In response, Joseph decided to get five lines tattooed on his right arm (see Tattoo #7 below). For him, the line tattoos represented a statement against the belief that tattoos are inappropriate in the workplace. He reiterated that he wanted to be more of a rebel. It was Joseph's way of declaring that "I have tattoos and you do not know it." Tattoos were a way for him to claim and accept himself. He experienced the coloured lines on his skin as being a part of himself.

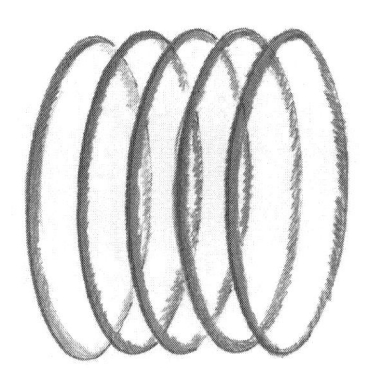

Tattoo 7

As a symbol, the line often represents a way of guiding a course of action, as in the way a mason hangs up his plumb line. As soon as the mason has hung it up, the work is guided without the continual need to look at the plumb line.[67] The line has also come to symbolize an ethical or moral benchmark, as in someone doing something that "crosses the line." For Joseph, the lines represented that very thing,

---

[67] Jean Chevalier and Alain Gheerbrant, *The Penguin Dictionary of Symbols*, p. 610.

as the workplace culture crossed the line when they dictated to their employees that tattoos were inappropriate in the workplace. Hence, for Joseph, the lines tattooed on his right forearm were his way of accepting himself and of creating a persona that rebelled against societal intolerance and close-mindedness toward those that were different and outside the norm. The line tattoos held a special place amongst his tattoos. To this point, the line tattoo was the only tattoo on his right arm. Joseph indicated that he wanted the coloured lines to artistically stand on their own. However, it was possible that the psychological importance of this tattoo was also associated with the ethical importance it reflected and that by having it stand alone he was highlighting just that.

The five coloured lines wrap around the forearm. As each line connected to form a circle, they were five mandalas, as stated previously. Joseph did not make the connection that the five lines became circles. Once again, as with the key tattoo, it was as if Joseph unconsciously selected the mandala image to calm and quell his inner emotional disturbance regarding the termination of a fellow employee. The work situation he was in at the time would have been stressful for him. He was directed by a superior to fire an employee for reasons that violated his own moral standards. The anxiety of the workplace situation led to his experiencing an impulse from the Self, to protect and calm his ego. That the mandala appeared immediately after the key tattoo seemed to validate the proposition that Joseph had unconsciously found the psychological key to protecting and reassuring his anxious ego by incorporating the mandala into his tattoos.

The fact that there are five lines, and not two or three or some other number, is symbolically significant from a qualitative perspective, but what does it mean in this context? For the Chinese, the number five represents the following:

> In China, the number five possesses the same significance as the four does for us because it is taken to represent the centered four. This concept is also found in the West, in the alchemical idea of the *quinta essentia*. The *quinta essentia* is not additively joined onto

the first four as a fifth element but represents the most refined spiritually imaginable unity of the four elements. It is either initially present in and extracted from, or produced by the circulation of these elements amongst one another. Whereas the pentagon with its five angles geometrizes the number five in its quantitative and additive form, the quintessence is represented by the quincunx as the centre of four.[68]

This refining of the potential for wholeness is the task assigned to the ego in individuation. Finally, the coloured lines have psychological connotations. It was likely that Joseph, with his finely tuned aesthetic sense, picked the colours of the five lines to satisfy his artistic taste. However, from a psychological perspective, the vibrancy of the colours suggested they may reflect the intensity of feelings and thoughts associated with the image and possibly symbolize that his heart, mind, body, spirit and soul were fully engaged with the tattoo.

In his twenty-fifth year, Joseph finally acquired the Hermes tattoo that he had wanted at the age of twenty (see Tattoo #8 below). We previously discussed how the impulse to tattoo an image of Hermes, like the initial clown tattoo, derived from the archetype of the trickster, but that it also reflected a psychological shift. On the persona level, the adolescent ego's identification with the clownish rebel trickster transitioned to a more mature and intellectual perspective. The tattoo artist had wanted a more aggressive depiction of Hermes while Joseph had wanted a softer portrayal of the image. Ultimately, he got the image he wanted. According to Joseph, the artistic rendition of Hermes had imperfections but he grew to accept and enjoy the tattoo.

---

[68] Marie-Louise von Franz, *Number and Time*, pp. 120-121.

Tattoo 8

The tattoo of Hermes, placed on the lower left arm, had him wearing the winged helmet or *petasos* that is associated with Hermes as the messenger of the gods.[69] A hat is round and fits on the head. Jung suggests the circular hat symbolizes a mandala.[70] He describes in *Dream Symbols of the Individuation Process* that when one puts on a hat, one comes under the influence of what it represents:

> In our case we can assume that by putting on the hat the dreamer will pass under a peculiar influence, presumably the influence of the unconscious, and will enter a new world of experience, namely, the experience of the collective unconscious. That is, he will be surrounded, invaded, influenced by ideas or events that come up from the lower levels, up from the basic structure of the mind.[71]

---

[69] Hermes. (2024, September 23). In *Wikipedia.* en.wikipedia.org/wiki/Hermes
[70] C.G. Jung, *Dream Symbols of the Individuation Process,* p. 313.
[71] Ibid., p. 79.

Therefore, the winged hat worn by Hermes symbolized that Joseph was coming under the archetypal influence represented by the winged messenger. That the image was only of Hermes's head suggested that Joseph identified more with the intellectual and creative aspect of Hermes, and at least not at this point, with a full depiction of the symbol of Hermes holding a caduceus with a snake coiled around it. The soft image showed the head surrounded by green vegetation and red flowers. Again, encircling the head with flowers suggested the ego was experiencing the protective and healing aspects of the mandala.

Joseph obtained another tattoo in his twenty-fifth year; namely, that of a beautiful red flower (see Tattoo #9 below). The flower image was situated just below the Hermes tattoo on the left arm. He stipulated that he acquired the image for its beauty and aesthetic impact, asserting there was no meaning for him beyond that. While discussing this particular image, Joseph recounted his longstanding self-esteem issues. He described himself as a "skinny, gay man." At that age he said he wanted people to know that it was okay for a gay man to adopt and value an aesthetic perspective. This particular tattoo made him feel really good.

Tattoo 9

At twenty-five, Joseph continued to be challenged by self-esteem issues. These issues manifested in the anxieties and insecurities experienced by the ego. Although he denied there was any meaning in the flower tattoo beyond that of aesthetics, it was remarkable that after making this denial, he proceeded to talk about his self-esteem issues. Without making a connection between the aesthetics and his self-esteem issues, he chose a beautiful image from nature to compensate for his anxieties and insecurities (which likely made him feel not so beautiful). The fact that he felt really good after acquiring the tattoo would seem to reinforce that proposition. Nonetheless, from a persona perspective, the ego identified with the beauty of the flower to make an aesthetic, artistic statement to others.

Below are comments from *The Book of Symbols* related to the flower as a natural mandala:

> The simplest form of the flower with a radial shape is a natural mandala linking the flower symbolically with the wheel and eternal cosmic movement around a mystic and orienting center. The flower's hermaphroditic qualities suggest the joining of opposites in self-becoming. Visible above yet rooted in the invisible below, the flower symbolically bridges the manifest and the unseen worlds, realms of latency and potentiality and those of active generation.[72]

This is the basis of our argument that the impulse for the flower tattoo originated from the Self, as a compensation for the ego's insecurities and anxieties. The ego, not feeling grounded within the psyche, responded to an impulse that grew naturally from the soil of its unconscious foundation.

Up to this point, we have not discussed the anima aspect of Joseph's tattoos. As previously noted, the anima archetype symbolizes the inner feminine aspect within a man's psyche. The anima's function is to filter the contents of the collective unconscious through to the ego. It was Joseph's anima that filtered the healing and supportive

---

[72] Ami Ronnenberg and Kathleen Martin, Eds, *The Book of Symbols – Reflections on Archetypal Images* (Cologne, Germany: Taschen, 2010) pp. 150-152.

mandala images through to his ego. For instance, the positive psychological characteristics of the feminine are to hold, contain and support. It was these very qualities that the mandala unconsciously provided to Joseph's insecure and anxious ego. Joseph's commitment to the artistic and aesthetic rendering of the tattoo images was attributable to the influence of the anima upon the ego. Additionally, the anima's influence was visible in the selection of Joseph's flower images, and the colour, flowing lines and softness they exude.

At the age of twenty-eight, Joseph acquired his seventh tattoo (see Tattoo #10). The tattoo was an image of a boxer on his upper left arm. He mentioned that prior to acquiring the tattoo, he had been going through a difficult emotional time with the recent breakup of a relationship.

Tattoo 10

He and a female friend, who is a tattooist, chose the image. The image was a stylized pose of a southpaw boxer appearing much like a boxer would in the nineteenth century. There were two orbs encircling the area around the boxer's head. Of note were tattoos on the boxer's body. On the boxer's left shoulder was what appears to be a dagger plunged into an image of a heart. On the right arm of the boxer was another knife that appeared to pierce the boxer's skin. There was an anchor on the boxer's left forearm along with what appears to be an image of a star placed on the bicep. Tattooed over the area of the boxer's heart was the word LOVE.

Prior to acquiring the boxer tattoo, Joseph's ego was going through an emotionally turbulent time. In an attempt to weather this difficult time, the ego identified with the fighting spirit of the boxer for assistance in getting through it. The boxer image situated just below the left shoulder represented the persona the ego identified with and was now presenting to the outside world.

The image of the boxer symbolized the archetype of the warrior. The inner warrior was a compensatory response from the instinctual foundation of the unconscious to the anxious, insecure, heartbroken and suffering ego in need of the fighter's spirit to stabilize and strengthen itself. That the impulse for this tattoo originated from the Self was evidenced by the two orbs encircling the head. These mandala images were the protective and healing effects emanating from the Self to the ego. The inner orb was red and likely symbolized the need to calm and quell the emotional storm assailing the suffering ego and the injury to its feeling function. The outer orb was larger, consisting of a circle of green leaves. Again, this image from nature likely symbolized a warm embrace encircling the ego from the protective natural aspect of the Self.

The multiple tattoos on the boxer's body represented the psychological storyline of Joseph's ego during this emotionally trying time. The image of the dagger plunging into a heart symbolized the emotional pain he was experiencing with the breakup of the relationship. As well, the knife piercing the skin on the boxer's other arm symbolized the piercing nature of the suffering undergone by the ego. During this difficult situation, the response of the ego was to harness its instinctual warrior's spirit and fight for its health and wellbeing, for its survival. By doing so, the ego harnessed the strength to fight for LOVE of himself, so that Joseph could get through this emotional upheaval and move forward with life.

The stylized nature of the boxer tattoo represented the emphasis Joseph placed on the artistic and aesthetic rendering of a tattoo. The two orbs surrounding the boxer's head were part of the artistic embellishment to enhance the aesthetics of the boxer image. The focus Joseph placed on the aesthetics of the tattoo, to the exclusion of the psychological perspective, prevented him from realizing some of its psychological aspects. For instance, the symmetry and beauty of the two orbs assisted the ego to feel better, a positive psychological effect the aesthetics of the tattoo had on the ego. However, Joseph was not aware of the psychological reason for his continuing to incorporate the mandala design in his tattoos; for example, why choose the two orbs? As noted before, the number two has to do psychologically with threshold phenomena. This means that unconscious content is either on the verge of crossing over into consciousness or needs to cross over into consciousness. A possible explanation for the two orbs was the need for Joseph's ego to become psychologically aware of the meaning of the mandala image and why Joseph repeatedly made use of it. The meaning of the mandala is that it occurs primarily when someone is experiencing psychological crisis, confusion and disorientation.

Joseph obtained his eighth tattoo in his twenty-eighth or twenty-ninth year (see Tattoo #11 below). The image was that of a skull located adjacent to the Hermes tattoo on the left arm. It was connected to his respect for and admiration of the Mexican culture. He had just moved to Toronto and did not speak any English. Joseph indicated this tattoo was very important to him. It represented family and anchored him like a family. For Joseph, the Mexican culture was about living life in a more relaxed way and enjoying the warmth of the sun. The Mexican way of life contrasted with his initial experience of Toronto and its relentless hustle and bustle. He related that the Mexican skull tattoo had a great psychological impact on him. The tattoo was a constant reminder that he came to Toronto and was able to make the necessary adjustments in order to adapt.

Tattoo 11

On top of the pain Joseph was experiencing due to the recent breakup of a romantic relationship, was the added stress of adjusting to a new city and a new language. Anxiety and insecurity were everyday challenges for Joseph. It wasn't surprising that his ego identified with an image that resonated with a more relaxed way of life. The skull was adorned with flowers and radiated a positive energy associated with the Mexican Day of the Dead, which is not a day of sadness but rather a festive one where family members celebrate those who have passed away.[73] It was the relaxed attitude of the Mexicans towards not only death but also all aspects of life that resonated with Joseph. It was this relaxed attitude that the persona identified with and wanted to project to the world.

---

[73] Day of the Dead. (2024, October 2). In *Wikipedia.* en.wikipedia.org/wiki/Day_of_the_Dead

Once again, the impulse experienced by the ego was a compensatory response from the Self to the anxious and insecure ego. Also, the mandala image of the flower between the skull's two eye sockets symbolized the protective, healing, and ordering aspect of the Self that the ego unconsciously tapped into in order to assuage its suffering during this time of stress and disorientation. It is noteworthy that a conscious psychological reference for Joseph was that the tattoo was a representation of the warmth he associated with family. As the reader might remember, Joseph's description of the impact of his own family on his psychological development was that it left him feeling very insecure, very afraid and very unhappy. Hence, the Mexican skull tattoo became a symbolic substitute for the joy, happiness and support he did not experience with his biological family. However, while Joseph was consciously anchoring himself with the Mexican tattoo, he was unconscious of the fact that he was also anchoring the ego inwardly by connecting to the protective and positive influence of the Self. The tattoo of the skull, connecting him to the Self, symbolized the inner anchoring and support he needed.

Also, the skull can be viewed as a symbol representing the land of the dead and the collective unconscious. The two black eye sockets encircled by flowers symbolized that perspective. The placement of the flower mandala between the two eye sockets symbolizes the third eye, as described in the following:

> Ajna (third eye) - is the sixth primary chakra in the body according to Hindu tradition. It is supposedly a part of the brain which can be made more powerful through meditation, yoga and other spiritual practices just as a muscle is. In Hindu tradition, it signifies the subconscious mind, the direct link to the brahman. While the person's two eyes see the physical world the third eye is believed to reveal insights about the future. The third eye chakra is said to connect people to their intuition, give them the ability to communicate with the world, or help them receive messages from the past and the future.[74]

---

[74] Ajna, *Wikipedia,* the free encyclopedia.

In connection to the above, where the third eye represents the capacity for an individual to receive messages via their intuition, it is worth remembering that Jung defines intuition as perception via the unconscious. Hence, the skull tattoo with its symbolic connection to the land of the dead and the symbolism associated with its two black eye sockets surrounded by flowers are, indeed, meaningful. The third eye flower mandala symbolizes the perspective afforded the ego from the collective unconscious. Joseph was unaware of these symbolic connections.

At the age of thirty-one, Joseph got his ninth tattoo (see Tattoo #12 below). It was the image of a diamond on the left wrist. He stated the tattoo was not of good quality and only cost twenty dollars. The tattoo was a mnemonic reminder of a relationship he had had with a man he described as a sociopath totally devoid of empathy. Joseph indicated that he associated the image with this man, who would treat Joseph like a diamond periodically. However, for the most part, the man played mind games which always resulted in his trying to manipulate and control Joseph. Joseph wanted the diamond image to be a permanent reminder of that relationship so as to prevent him from repeating the same mistake.

Tattoo 12

The diamond, as a symbol, is basically associated with positive qualities. It is considered the most precious of precious stones. For some, it symbolizes light and life, faithfulness and everlasting love, immutability, sincerity, purity and immortality. Psychologically, the diamond symbolizes the pinnacle of development and fulfillment, being associated with the alchemists' myth of the "philosopher's stone."[75] As such, the diamond symbolizes the archetype of the Self. Therefore, it was interesting that Joseph connected the image to negative memories.

The diamond tattoo had multiple reference points for Joseph. It reminded him of the bad relationship with the partner who would periodically treat Joseph like a diamond, but without real love and empathy. At the same time, the purpose of the mnemonic reminder was to prod the ego into remaining conscious and to not succumb to the charms of such a destructive personality in the future. As the positive aspects of the diamond are associated with the Self, it is likely Joseph projected aspects of the Self onto this past partner. The projection would have prevented Joseph from truly seeing the pathological personality of this person with whom he was involved. With the passage of time and the accumulation of sufficient experience, the projection had receded, exposing the true nature of the man.

It was likely the impulse from the Self was compensatory in nature, prodding the ego to increased psychological awareness and likely, Joseph was partially aware of this call to greater consciousness when he used the diamond tattoo as a mnemonic reminder. He was nudging himself to be more vigilant so as to prevent falling under the influence of another pathological personality. Joseph's spending of the paltry sum of twenty dollars on a valuable diamond seemed to epitomize the anger he held, both towards his ex-partner and himself. In the final analysis, Joseph felt betrayed by the ex-lover and possibly by his own lack of awareness.

Joseph considered the diamond tattoo to be a poor technical rendition of the image. He had a fine aesthetic appreciation of artistic quality.

---

[75] Hans Biederman, *Dictionary of Symbolism* (New York, Penguin Books, 1994) p. 95.

However, to a casual observer, the image appeared as a beautiful diamond. The development of ego consciousness is a process informed by the pain and suffering that comes with life. Wisdom is defined as the quality of having experience, knowledge, and good judgement.[76] If Joseph learns to value wisdom and seeks to develop those qualities within himself, it is possible his perspective regarding the diamond will deepen and shift. While this tattoo will always carry the negative mnemonic reference he attributed to it, if he acquires wisdom along the way, in time he may come to realize how much he actually values the positive aspects of the diamond as a symbol. As the alchemists suggest, it represents the ultimate in psychological development, the "diamond body" and "the philosopher's stone." The practical commencement of this lifelong process is the ego's realization that the archetype of the Self, the central regulating archetype of the collective unconscious, is the impulse behind this development which has the potential to aid and abet it along the way.

Joseph's tenth tattoo came in his thirty-second year (see Tattoo #13). He stated there was no story behind the image of a lion on his left shoulder. He just liked the aesthetics of the lion image and had wanted a larger tattoo on the left shoulder. Again, even though he denied a story related to the image, it caused him to experience a big boost to his self-esteem, which he still felt a year later when he participated in the study.

---

[76] *The Concise Oxford Dictionary of Current English*, eighth edition, Ed. R.E. Allen, p. 1407.

Tattoo 13

As Joseph did not provide any associations with respect to the meaning the lion had for him, we drew on connotations which various cultures have attributed to this animal. Barbara Hannah, a close friend and colleague of Jung's, delivered a series of lectures at the C.G. Jung Institute in Zurich, Switzerland, concerning the archetypal symbolism of animals. Her 1958 lecture, specifically related to the image of lion, breaks the symbolism of the lion into four classes: a solar symbol, a symbol of power, a symbol of urge, desire, and passion, and a symbol of resurrection and spiritual mana.[77]

The tenth tattoo closely followed the diamond tattoo. The lion image was located on the left shoulder just above the boxer tattoo, which was also connected to the termination of a romantic relationship. It was noteworthy that the head of the lion was not confined to the left shoulder, but extended to the area of the chest adjacent to the heart. The image of the lion appears to be roaring. Hannah refers to the forceful impact of the lion's roar:

---
[77] Barbara Hannah, *The Archetypal Symbolism of Animals*, p. 24.

> Certainly, the lion's roar has an extraordinary effect and undoubtedly forms a part of the reason why it is regarded as the king of the beasts. I once had a flat not far from Regent's Park and used to hear the lions roaring early in the morning before the traffic began and, although I knew they were safely behind bars, it certainly was a bloodcurdling sound.[78]

Even though Joseph remarked there was no story behind the selection of the lion image, other than the aesthetics of the tattoo, he did acknowledge a lasting boost to his self-esteem. The beauty of the image alone could not account for a such a lengthy psychological effect. It was more likely the ego unconsciously selected the lion to create a more instinctual, dynamic persona to compensate for its anxieties and insecurities. The kingly roar of the lion symbolizes the capacity to ward off any potential threats. Also, that the roar of the lion was directed towards the area of the heart and was situated above the boxer, suggested to us that the ego was instinctively trying to protect and preserve the feelings associated with the heart.

The lion represented a noteworthy shift in the nature of Joseph's image selection. Many of the images selected to this point were filtered through the lens of Joseph's love and respect for aesthetics, the imagination, the arts and the intellect. With the boxer image, we witnessed the introduction of the instinctual, fighter spirit. The lion represented a further deepening of the ego's unconscious need to strengthen and protect itself by drawing on the animal, instinctual, dynamic nature of the collective unconscious. The impulse that issued from the Self was a compensatory response to the anxious and vulnerable ego and ticked off all four boxes in Hannah's symbolic classification of the lion.

Firstly, the lion has symbolic connections to the sun and its influence. As Hannah notes,

> Leo is the well-known zodiacal sign for the days from July 24 to August 23, the hottest time of the year. We should bear in mind

---

[78] Ibid., p. 273.

that these symbols arose in a hotter climate than ours where the heat from July to August is formidable.[79]

From a psychological perspective, this has to do with consciousness. Joseph said the lion was chosen solely for its aesthetic effect. He simply wanted the beautiful image tattooed onto his skin. Joseph was unconscious of the degree to which his emotions were constellated. The lion, in this instance, symbolizes the emotional response from the instinctual aspect of his psyche to heal and protect his broken heart. This is an ultraviolet aspect of the lion image that he needs to become aware of in time. At the same time, Joseph needed to become aware of not allowing the negative aspects affiliated with the symbol, i.e., rage and other destructive emotions, to overtake and possess the ego.

The fiery lion has so much to do symbolically with the emotions. And without the emotions nothing is fruitful. We learn a lot in psychology that remains in the cold intellectual realm, for nothing really counts psychologically until the emotions are involved. Even negative emotions, I should say, are preferable to none. Emotions can be called the fertile ground of our psyche, which is why it is so preferable to cultivate them.[80]

Another meaning attributed to the archetype of the lion is that of power, the second quality Hannah cites in her classification scheme. The insecure, anxious ego, consistently plagued by fears, needed to become aware of an unconscious identification with the roaring lion image because of its association with power. Thirdly, the ego unconsciously identified with the other meanings symbolized by the lion; namely, those having to do with urge, desire and passion. Hence, as we noted previously, the lion's location above the boxer and in the vicinity of the heart was significant. Joseph's ego needed to become conscious that it was identified with an image related to the ideas of desire and passion in order to compensate for recent injuries in the arena of love. Fourthly, the ego needed to become aware that because of this identification, it was aligning itself with

---

[79] Barbara Hannah, *The Archetypal Symbolism of Animals*, p. 275.
[80] Ibid. p. 276.

hope for the transformation of the ego from insecurity and anxiety toward confidence, authority and prestige.

We could ask why the lion image manifested at this time, rather than ten years earlier, as surely the insecure and anxious ego could have benefitted from the positive aspects of the lion symbol then? Like most things in life, it has to do with timing and the readiness of Joseph's ego to accept the meanings and instinctual energies represented by the lion. Jung speaks to this in the following passage from Hannah in *The Archetypal Symbolism of Animals*:

> This system of images is also born in human beings, it is the archetypes, the potential force in man, but it only comes to surface when the moment for it is ripe, then the archetype functions as an urge, like an instinct. In the collective unconscious the archetypes and instincts are one and the same thing.[81]

The chronology and sequence of Joseph's tattoos reflected a gradual psychological transition from abstract and intellectual designs to those more representative of nature and the instincts. This suggests to us that the compensatory response from the collective unconscious was attempting to balance the intellectual ego by connecting it to the instincts. This transition continued with Joseph's most recent tattoo.

Joseph got his eleventh tattoo in his thirty-third year (see Tattoo #14 below). He described it as an image representing a warrior. He once again said the image had no specific meaning or relevance for him. He simply liked the aesthetics of it. The tattoo was a large piece located on the right thigh. The image consists of a warrior's head surrounded by two animal images, one above the warrior's head, the other below. The animal image covering the skull area of the warrior was the upper part of the head of an animal resembling a fox or wolf. The animal image from below the jaw area was a skull of some unidentifiable animal. Though we were unable to identify the specific animal represented by the lower image, it definitely exudes a ferocious energy, which was very much in keeping with warrior

---

[81] Ibid., p. 145.

spirit. It was interesting that the warrior in this image had the same stylized moustache as in the boxer tattoo.

Tattoo 14

Again, the impulse for the warrior tattoo originated from the collective unconscious, specifically the archetype of the warrior and the central archetype, the Self. That the Self was involved was evidenced by the garland of red flowers encircling the entire image. As previously cited, individual flowers symbolize a mandala. When placed symmetrically as a garland surrounding the warrior image, these flowers also form a mandala.

The head of the human warrior was covered by what seemed to be a wolf head indicating Joseph was unconscious of the fact that his ego was identified with the symbolism of the wolf. In addition, Joseph was unaware of the skull symbolism below his jaw area. Both images had to do with the spirit of the warrior and the insecure and anxious ego was unconsciously trying to connect to the spirit of the warrior. The lower image of an animal skull exuded a more ferocious quality than the upper wolf image. The meaning of both animal skulls, however, relates to the ultraviolet aspect of the warrior archetype.

Periodically in our discussion of Joseph's tattoos, we have alluded to the need for him, over time, to become conscious of the ultraviolet aspect, which is the meaning contained within the archetypal image. This need to become conscious of the ultraviolet aspect of the image applies to all the images tattooed on his body, not just the ones specifically mentioned in this chapter. As discussed earlier, the infrared aspect of the archetype, the mode of action, is the tattoo itself, the action taken by the ego in response to the impulse from the instinctual infrastructure within the archetype.

Joseph wore his tattoos proudly. He said he wanted to be part of the process of normalizing the tattoo, both in the larger community and in the workplace. The aesthetics of a tattoo mattered most to him; however, at times he was aware of a psychological component to his tattoos. We have suggested psychological components of which Joseph was not conscious. Beyond the beauty of his tattoos, which did provide a boost to his self-esteem, the chronological sequence of the tattoos reflected a compensatory impulse from the collective unconscious to protect and assist an anxious and insecure ego. The transition to animal images suggested the central archetype of the unconscious was trying to compensate and support an ego that heavily relied on the intellect and the artistic imagination for orientation in the world. The repeated manifestation of the mandala theme in his tattoos reflected the protective and healing aspect of the Self, providing the ego with an ongoing sense of reassurance and support.

Sophie

"Sophie" is a pseudonym. Sophie was twenty-seven years old at the time of her interview for the study. She was living with her girlfriend and two cats. She had enjoyed learning and her time spent in the academic milieu. Her first degree gave her the realization she could not save the world. Her second degree allowed her to work in a profession that improves the human condition, one person at a time. She stated she had had a good childhood and family experience. She has a brother eleven years her senior. She said everyone knew she was an "accident," as her parents were in their forties when she was born. She also said both she and her brother grew up with "single child syndrome," as the eleven-year age difference between them resulted in each feeling they had no sibling to whom they could relate.

She indicated both parents worked long hours, so she was mostly raised by her maternal grandmother. Her grandmother was a good cook with a good sense of humour, who raised Sophie as though she were her own daughter. Sophie reported that she had other people to interact with, as her grandmother had raised a number of her cousins and other relations as well. She told of her grandma plunking everyone down in front of the television. In recent years with her grandmother's health deteriorating, Sophie's mother had been spending a lot of her free time looking after her. Sophie herself made a point of visiting her grandmother at least once a week.

She described her father as a workaholic who supported her financially but not emotionally. She had not had a good relationship with him until recently. The father was described as quiet in nature. He let his wife do the raising of the kids and the running of the household. She remembered him taking a backseat in the household, although she had a lasting memory that he loved to go grocery shopping. He was now retired and, according to Sophie, needed a hobby as he had too much time on his hands.

Sophie painted a picture of a mother of Italian heritage who was very loud and partially deaf. She was described as very "cool," an extraverted personality who was socially adept. An example of mother being "cool": although she was described as strict, she was relaxed enough to allow her daughter to have parties/drinking at the home where she could monitor the situation. Sophie recollected that her mother did everything in the home.

Sophie had to go to church until the age of sixteen. She had not gone since. Her father was an altar boy when he was young. He had not attended church since that time. Her mother went to church every Sunday. Sophie indicated that neither of her parents had mental health nor substance abuse issues.

Sophie believed much of her personality had been shaped by her mother. She described herself as a loud, strong-willed woman. Neither parent had ever told her they loved her, but despite this, she felt loved by them. She disclosed that neither parent had ever hugged her either. To this day she does not want to be hugged and cannot hug others. Sophie had been told by her girlfriend/friends that she was emotionally cold and distant. Sophie thought that she used her easygoing personality and sense of humour as a deflection.

Since the age of sixteen, Sophie had spent her free time doing roller derby because she had a friend who did not like to party, so this was a sober activity to do with her. She reported having had multiple physical injuries from the sport, such as black eyes and injured knees, but that she loved it nonetheless. She also enjoyed going to the gym and to concerts. She described herself as an extraverted personality who was loud and funny and who enjoyed spending time with large social groups. She felt she was satisfied with her life.

At age seventeen, Sophie had an impulse to get a tattoo. She went to one tattoo shop, but the tattooist there told her she was foolish for wanting to get a tattoo at her age. She then went to another tattooist and had her mother sign off on the tattoo. Her first tattoo was an image of the number sixteen. She selected the number sixteen as she wanted to celebrate her birthday which is on October 16th. She had other positive associations to the number, but did not share them. The tattoo was situated in the neck area just below the back of her left ear. She was not really sure why she chose that part of the body other than that she could hide the tattoo behind her hair. The image was done in white and is now quite faded. She recalled getting the tattoo primarily for the 'cool' factor. The tattoo process itself also had significance as it felt really cool sharing the experience with a friend. She said there was no psychological reason for getting the number sixteen tattoo other than to celebrate her birthday. Sophie also maintained that obtaining the tattoo had no impact on her psychological attitude and she did not feel any different after getting one. The tattoo was a good catalyst for conversation with her friends. Her initial tattoos were hidden because her mother did not like visible tattoos.

Tattoo 15

Sophie said she chose the number sixteen as an affirmative daily reminder that her birth was something to positively celebrate, not just an "accident." Also, though she dismissed any sense of a psychological change accompanying the acquisition of the tattoo, Sophie's acknowledgment of the "cool" factor suggested her persona/ego experienced a sense of doing something interesting and exciting. Her tattoo seemed to have brought, temporarily at least, a charismatic sparkle to her conversation with friends.

Having shared Sophie's associations with the tattoo, we now look at it through a Jungian lens to see if there might be additional layers of meaning. As in the previous chapters, we will start by examining her impulse to get the tattoo and what the psychological implications of that impulse might be. In order to formulate our hypothesis, we need to remind ourselves of some vital components of Sophie's personality and the family context that played a part in its development. Just as she had described her mother, Sophie described herself as having an extraverted personality. Jung defines extraversion as follows:

> Extraversion is an outward-turning of libido (q.v.). I use this concept to denote a manifest relation of subject to object, a positive movement of subjective interest towards the object. Everyone in the extraverted state thinks, feels, and acts in relation to the object, and moreover in a direct and clearly observable fashion, so that no doubt can remain about his positive dependence on the object. In a sense, therefore, extraversion is a transfer of interest from subject to object.[82]

Sophie's belief that she was extraverted was confirmed by the details she provided of herself and her behaviour. For example, she asserted that she felt most at home in large social groups. This example demonstrated she habitually transferred interest/energy from subject to object. Further, she mentioned that her first academic degree focused on International Studies because she had an interest in solving the problems of the larger world. Again, this illustrated that Sophie continuously transfers her energy outwardly to the world. Eventually, when she came to the realization that she could not solve the world's problems, she continued to channel her energy in an extraverted direction, though on a smaller scale. These examples emphasize that Sophie regularly directed her energy towards extraverted interests, activities and occupations.

Sophie was seventeen when she acquired the numerical tattoo. She had reached the age at which individual personalities transition from adolescence to adulthood. This psychological truth was even

---

[82] C.G. Jung, *Psychological Types*, Collected Works, Vol. 6 (Princeton University Press, 1972), p. 427.

enshrined in law. For example, in the province of Ontario, Canada, where Sophie lives, persons who are 16 years of age or older can legally withdraw from parental or caregiver control and leave home.[83] This suggests society recognizes a developmental phase has been reached at that age that allows one to care for oneself. Hence, the age at which Sophie obtained the numerical tattoo was significant from a developmental and psychological perspective. She was transitioning from adolescence to adulthood psychologically.

The number sixteen is composed of two numbers, the number one and the number six. We will first explore the qualitative aspect of the number one. Jung explained that the number one contains all the succeeding numbers: "One is the first from which all other numbers arise, and in which the opposite qualities of numbers, the odd and the even, must therefore be united..."[84] The number one represents preconscious or potential wholeness, the *unus mundus*, or "one world." Jung writes that "the division into two was necessary in order to bring the "one" world out of the state of potentiality into reality. Reality consists of a multiplicity of things. But one is not a number; the first number is two, and with it multiplicity and reality begin."[85]

Jung attributes a generative aspect to the number six when discussing its qualitative component: "Nevertheless, it should not be forgotten that the number six (the *senarius*) was considered in ancient times "aptissimus generationi" (most fit for generation)." [86] When discussing the alchemical pictures in the *Psychology of the Transference*, Jung refers in a footnote to the generative aspect of the number six:

> The number six is most skilled in begetting, for it is even and uneven, partaking both of the active nature on account of the uneven, and of the hylical nature on account of the even, for which

---

[83] jfcy.org
[84] C.G. Jung, *Psychology and Religion*, Collected Works, Vol.11 (Princeton, Princeton University Press, 1975), p. 118.
[85] C.G. Jung, *Mysterium Coniunctionis*, Collected Works, Vol. 14 (Princeton, Princeton University Press, 1974), p. 462.
[86] C.G. Jung, *Alchemical Studies*, Collected Works, Vol. 13 (Princeton, Princeton University Press, 1970), p. 266.

reason the ancients also named it marriage and harmony...It leads to like-mindedness and friendship, giving health to the body, harmony to songs and music, virtue to the soul, prosperity to the state, and forethought to the universe.[87]

What is noteworthy about this reference is that it is incorporated into Jung's discussion of the transference. The transference by its very nature is an unconscious phenomenon that until resolved gets in the way of conscious relationship. This quality of the number six in the context of the transference suggests that when activated it has a generative quality which alerts the ego to the need for generating conscious relationship.

The illustration of the white number sixteen was encircled by a pink background. The pink is not part of the tattoo. The illustrator did this in order for the number to be more clearly visible to the viewer. The actual white tattoo became quite faded. This led us to ask about the significance of the colour white. White can symbolize a multitude of things. Depending on the context and culture, it can symbolize purity, innocence, death, ghostly apparitions, the spirit and much more. It can be either positive or negative.[88] In alchemical imagery, Jung explains that white (*albedo*) symbolizes the second stage of the psychological process, a cleansing of the individual's psychological shadow, (*nigredo*), the first stage of a development towards consciousness and the light of illumination: "From the darkness of the unconscious comes the light of illumination, the albedo. The opposites are contained in it in potential, hence the hermaphroditism of the unconscious, its capacity for spontaneous and autochthonous reproduction."[89]

In trying to track down the latent meaning of the numerical tattoo, it was crucial to remember that it was meaningfully situated just below

---

[87] C.G. Jung, *The Practice of Psychotherapy*, Collected Works, Vol. 16 (Princeton, Princeton University Press, 1975), p. 238.
[88] Hans Biedermann, *Dictionary of Symbolism*, (New York: Meridian, 1994), p. 380.
[89] C.G. Jung, *Mysterium Coniunctionis*, Collected Works, Vol. 14 (Princeton: Princeton University Press, 1974), p. 177.

the left ear, on a diagonal angle, as if pointing towards it. The function of the ear is that it facilitates hearing, it's a physiological function with numerous symbolic associations. There are two symbolic associations related to the ear in particular that are relevant. The first association is that the ear is viewed in certain cultures as having spiritual connotations:

> The ear is the symbol of the receptive, passive aspect of communication, as distinct from its active transmissive side. At Pozan, in Burma, there is a very ancient statue of the Buddha receiving enlightenment through his ears, while St Paul's *fides ex auditu* explains that the faith handed down by oral tradition is received through hearing. The ear stands in this context as the womb, or at least as the channel of spiritual life.[90]

The second association is that the ear has symbolic connections to birth:

> Because of the resemblance between the external ear and the spiral coil of a snail's shell (in human anatomy, the word "helix" and "antihelix" are used), there came to be a symbolic association linking the ear, the snail, and birth (which resembled the emergence of the snail from its shell); it was said of some gods and demigods that they had been born from out of their mothers' ears.[91]

It is important to remember the context of this first tattoo. Sophie experienced the impulse to get a tattoo and went to a tattoo shop where the tattooist refused to give her a tattoo, saying she was foolish for doing so at her age. Not to be denied, Sophie got her mother to sign off on getting a tattoo with another tattooist. She got the number sixteen tattooed, celebrating the date of her birth. Sophie described herself as a strong-willed woman. The scenario surrounding the acquisition of the numerical tattoo confirmed she was. Once the impulse to get a tattoo was experienced by her, she made sure it happened.

---

[90] Jean Chevalier and Alain Gheerbrant, *The Penguin Dictionary of Symbols*, (New York: Penguin Books, 1996), p. 330.
[91] Hans Biedermann, *Dictionary of Symbolism*, (New York: Meridian, 1994), p. 110.

As in previous examples of tattoo impulses and image choice, the question needing to be posed is, "What does the impulse to get a tattoo have to do with Sophie psychologically?" Looking back, we recall Sophie informing us she was raised in a household where she felt loved, even though she was not explicitly told by either of her parents that they loved her. In addition, she cannot recollect either parent embracing or hugging her. Her parents for whatever reason were unable to express verbal and physical affection. However, Sophie did not point the finger of blame at her parents for their human shortcomings. She was fortunate to know she was loved, regardless. It is often common psychological maxim that the unlived life of the parents is visited upon the children. This truism was confirmed in Sophie's psychology. To this day she does not like to be hugged and said she could not hug others. In psychological parlance, Sophie developed a feeling-toned complex related to this issue.

Our hypothesis is that the numerical white tattoo meaningfully placed near the left ear had implications regarding the development of Sophie's personality. First of all, the age at which Sophie obtained the tattoo and the number sixteen in chronological terms suggested this. Also as mentioned before, Sophie has an extraverted personality. We postulate that an aspect of the ultraviolet meaning of the numerical image was the need for her to listen (ear) to the promptings of the self-regulatory centre of the psyche, the Self, and develop aspects of her personality that had been left undeveloped. Sophie had developed one of the two attitudinal types discerned by Jung, in her case extraversion.[92] What was now needed by her ego was to acknowledge the other attitudinal type, introversion, and direct energy towards developing those aspects of her personality. Jung defines introversion as follows:

> Introversion means an inward-turning of libido (q.v.), in the sense of a negative relation of subject to object. Interest does not move towards the object but withdraws from it in to the subject. Everyone whose attitude is introverted thinks, feels, and acts in a

---

[92] Marie-Louise von Franz, *Jung's Typology*, (Dallas: Spring Publications Inc., 1984), p. 1.

way that clearly demonstrates that the subject is the prime
motivating factor and that the object is of secondary importance.[93]

Psychologically, most people habitually do what comes naturally to them. Developing the extraverted function to adapt to the world was what came naturally to Sophie. Being with her friends was what allowed her to feel at home and comfortable in the world. However, even her friends told her she was distant and cold emotionally. Upon meeting Sophie, it was apparent she had a likeable and easygoing way of relating to others. She recognized that she used her easygoing manner and good sense of humour to deflect others from getting to know the inner woman, of letting them fully embrace her. She habitually kept distance between herself and others on the feeling side, refraining from hugging or embracing others, including her girlfriend. It was apparent that the difficulty in hugging was a feeling-toned complex that entrenched itself within her personality at an early age and regularly compromised her feeling response to others and herself.

The consequence of being so developed on the extraverted side of her personality was that she did not habitually try and resolve issues like the hugging complex by utilizing her thinking in an introverted manner to unpack the inner workings of the complex. Consequently, the unconscious tried to influence the ego on this issue by sending it a compensatory impulse for a tattoo. The meaning behind the image was that in order to resolve the hugging complex, Sophie would need to do an about-face and turn her gaze to her inner world.

Orientation to the left is commonly known in Jungian circles as representing the unconscious. For this reason, it is noteworthy that the white tattoo was situated behind the left ear. When we speak of the qualitative aspect of the number one as symbolizing preconscious wholeness and the number six as representing a begetting or generative factor, we were suggesting that the two numbers were meaningfully aligned to prompt Sophie to awaken and consciously initiate a psychological process of development. The message went

---

[93] C.G. Jung, *Psychological Types*, Collected Works, Vol. 6 (Princeton: Princeton University Press, 1972), pp. 452-453.

beyond developing the introverted aspect of her personality in order to resolve the hugging complex. That was a first step. Developing the introverted aspects of her personality would initiate a lifelong process of making conscious her preconscious potential for wholeness. Further psychological development for all of us lies with developing those parts of our personalities that have been left behind. Turning her ego's attention to the introverted aspects of her psyche would open Sophie to unexplored psychological potential. Until now, Sophie had always wanted to solve the problems of others. The impulse from the archetypal foundation of her psyche, the Self, was prompting her to turn inward and solve this psychological issue that compromised her adaptation to herself and others. The impulse was directing her to stop deflecting the issue.

We have already referred to the developmental significance of Sophie's age and the tattoo. The conscious process of psychological individuation is seldom undertaken with commitment at such a young age. Also, we must remember that she mentioned her mother did not like visible tattoos so she hid the tattoo under her hair. This is interesting due to one particular association with the symbolic meaning of hair, as described by von Franz: "Hair on the head represents unconscious thoughts — that's why hair has mana power. Sometimes we influence our environment much more by our unconscious thoughts. This is why hair, the spiritual power of our unconscious thoughts, is so important."[94] This suggests there were conflicting thoughts, conscious and unconscious, regarding the tattoo. The placement of the tattoo was strongly influenced by considerations of what the mother liked and disliked. The numerical tattoo itself celebrated Sophie's own thoughts related to the date of her birth. Nonetheless, the pre-eminent thing to remember is that Sophie wanted a tattoo of the number sixteen and that nothing was going to stop her from getting it. It is meaningful that at the age of sixteen Sophie made the decision to stop going to church and embraced the sport of roller derby, a sport she continues to love and participate in. So, while the hidden location of the tattoo symbolized

---

[94] Marie-Louise von Franz, *Introduction to the Interpretation of Fairy Tales*, Collected Works, Vol. 8 (Asheville: Chiron Publications, 2023), p. 207.

the influence of the mother with regard to the ego's decisions, Sophie's move to end her involvement with the church and adopt a sport she loved symbolized the birth of her becoming her own person. This suggested to us that the strength of the impulse from the Self had been heeded, unconsciously, and that in the course of time the unconscious, latent meaning of the tattoo may manifest itself.

Sophie got her next tattoo approximately a year later. She revealed that it was situated on the left side of the ribs and was also easily concealed. It was an image of the three-eyed fish, Blinky, from the satirical animated TV series, "The Simpsons". Set in the fictional town of Springfield, of no identifiable state, the weekly themes centre around the Simpson family. The father, Homer, works as a safety inspector at the local nuclear plant. He is depicted as a ridiculous sort of character, not really competent or responsible enough to fulfil his role at the plant. His incompetence is connected to the toxic waste that contaminates the local lake and rivers. Blinky is an orange, three-eyed fish discovered in the local river; its mutations cause public outrage about the contamination emitted by Homer's nuclear plant.[95] Sophie said that the tattoo had an environmental connotation for her. She emphasized her fondness for Homer's eight-year-old daughter Lisa, a character presented as a precocious feminist and activist who cares deeply about the environment.[96] Sophie again stated she did not feel any different after getting the second tattoo, and that the second tattoo had no noticeable difference or impact on her psychological attitude.

When looking after Sophie while the parents were working, her grandmother frequently put Sophie in front of the TV. In response to a question concerning the psychological relevance, if any, of watching "The Simpsons," Sophie indicated it was a big part of her childhood. The significance of the three-eyed fish from Sophie's perspective was that it referred to the need for society to awaken to the damage it was doing to the environment. This was the objective connotation of the fish symbol, the reference to the outer world.

---

[95] The Simpsons. (2024, October 7). In *Wikipedia*. en.wikipedia.org/wiki/The_Simpsons
[96] Ibid.

We will now consider the subjective component of the fish symbol, and what relevance it may have had to her inner psychological world. Von Franz has this to say about the psychological significance of the fish:

> Psychologically the fish is a distant, inaccessible content of the unconscious, a sum of potential energy loaded with possibilities but with a lack of clarity. It is a libido symbol of a relatively uncharacterized and unspecified amount of psychic energy, the direction and development of which are not yet outlined. The ambivalence regarding the fish derives from its being a content below the threshold of consciousness.[97]

Beyond its symbolizing unconscious contents, the image of the fish has been associated with Christ the Redeemer:

> In *Aion,* Jung deals extensively with the symbolism of Christ as the fish; reference can therefore be made to that work. In many religions the fish, as already mentioned, is chiefly a symbol of the redeemer, and has therefore also been equated with Christ. At the same time the extraordinary revival of fish symbolism in early Christianity is not without a synchronistic connection with the beginning of the astrological Age of the Fishes. The fish emerged at that time as an image of the depths of the unconscious and became associated with the figure of Christ. In a special sense, therefore, the fish represents that aspect of Christ which marks him as a content of the unconscious, a manifestation, as it were, of the unconscious Self.[98]

Before we can discuss the psychological relevance of the fish tattoo, we need first to describe the symbolic implication of some of its attributes. The eye is seen to represent consciousness: "The eye, like the sun, is a symbol as well as an allegory of consciousness."[99] Also, the eye is frequently referred to as being the proverbial "window of

---

[97] Marie-Louise von Franz, *Introduction to the Interpretation of Fairy Tales*, Collected Works, Vol. 8 (Asheville: Chiron Publications, 2023), p. 149.
[98] Emma Jung and Marie-Louise von Franz, *The Grail Legend*. (Boston: Sigo Press, 1986), p. 189.
[99] C.G. Jung, *Mysterium Coniunctionis*, Collected Works, Vol. 14 (Princeton: Princeton University Press, 1974), p. 53.

the soul." It is not surprising that the Egyptians held the belief that the eye is the seat of the soul.[100] Because a fish's eyes are always open, this is sometimes seen as representing the eye of God.[101] In Jungian terminology, this would translate as the eye symbolizing the all-seeing aspect of the psyche, the Self.

As the fish is orange, we need to explore some of the connotations of that colour. *The Book of Symbols* points out that orange is composed of red and yellow. Orange is often associated with the emerging and the descending sun. As such, orange can be associated with heat, growth, perfection and desire, and because it is linked to the foregoing qualities, it can be related to processes of maturation and transformation.[102]

Blinky had three eyes, an unnatural deviation from the normal two. It is noteworthy that in the Hindu religion the third eye is known as *Ajna* or third eye chakra which signifies "the unconscious mind, the direct link to Brahman."[103] Within the Hindu religion, Brahman represents the supreme authority and is known as "the Creator."[104]

The unconscious is like a river that runs beneath consciousness. As such, it responds to how the ego is living its life. The unconscious sends compensatory dreams to the ego that, if acknowledged, offer the ego the possibility of correcting an inadequate perspective. We suggest the impulse for a tattoo is another means used by the unconscious to compensate the ego's perspective and behaviour. It is also important for us to keep in mind that each subsequent tattoo is meaningfully connected to the preceding ones. The challenge for us is to discover the psychological connection among them. We maintain that Sophie's first tattoo represented a compensatory impulse from the unconscious foundation, the Self, offering the possibility for the ego to reconsider its predominantly extraverted

---

[100] Ibid., p. 52.
[101] Ibid., p. 51.
[102] *The Book of Symbols*, Ami Ronnberg, editor-in-chief (Cologne: Taaschen, 2010), p. 642.
[103] Ajna. (2024, September 7). In *Wikipedia.* en.wikipedia.org/wiki/Ajna
[104] Brahman. (2024, October 2). In *Wikipedia.* en.wikipedia.org/wiki/Brahman

perspective and consider giving some attention to the introverted side of the psyche, the inner world of the unconscious. A year later, the fish tattoo appeared. Our challenge then becomes not only decoding the latent meaning of the second tattoo, but also its psychological relationship to the first.

Blinky's three eyes were viewed as a negative mutation caused by exposure to nuclear waste. Subjectively, the fish symbolizes an unconscious content that has atrophied through the ego's neglect, like the nuclear waste appearing in the local water as result of poor supervision at the nuclear plant. The second tattoo suggested that the latent meaning of the first tattoo was carried into the second. The inner world of the psyche, the world of the unconscious, had not been tended to. Sophie continued to orient herself primarily towards the external world and neglect her inner world. Rather than balancing her attitudinal perspective by developing an introverted component, Sophie continued to predominantly orient herself through extraversion.

It is highly significant that the third eye is situated between the two physical eyes and that this is known within the Hindu religion as Ajna (or third eye chakra), signifying the unconscious mind. It is also seen as a direct link to Brahman, which in Jungian terminology correlates to the Self. This gives validity to the hypothesis that the Self, the self-regulating centre of the psyche, sent the impulse to the ego to acquire the fish tattoo. If this hypothesis is true, it suggests the ego still needs to recalibrate the way it orients itself within the psyche and out in the world.

As we have said, one of the connotations of the fish is that it symbolizes redemption. It is our viewpoint that redemption is an essential component latent within the fish symbol. Also, it is meaningful that the colour orange is related to the sunset and sunrise. The fish tattoo made manifest on the skin by the ego signals to the Jungian depth psychologist that the archetype of the Self is activated and wanting the ego's attention. The old attitude of merely adapting to the world via extraversion was the sunset aspect of the orange colour symbolically. The sunrise aspect of the orange colour related to the ego needing to include an introverted attitude within its perspective. The ego, by including an introverted attitude, would allow itself to discover the archetype of the Self, that is the redemptive, sunrise component of the colour orange.

A few years later Sophie experienced another impulse to get a tattoo. She was in another city competing in a roller derby competition. After the competition, she went to a tattoo shop. While Sophie discussed with the tattooist the image she wanted, the tattooist informed her that he was skilled at tattooing cacti. Sophie decided to go with the image of a cactus and had a small cactus tattooed on the right side of her ribs. Again, the tattoo was on a part of the body where it could be easily hidden. The tattoo had to be redone when she returned to her home city (as the tattooist had pressed too hard while tattooing the image and the ink bled out), but Sophie was very satisfied with the reworked image. She again said there was no noticeable change in her psychological attitude after getting the tattoo.

Tattoo 16

The cactus is indigenous to the Americas and is found for the most part in hot and dry environments. As a result, it adapts to environments where water is not plentiful by efficiently conserving and utilizing the little water that is available. The sharp protective spines that are a frequent feature of the cactus are botanically explained as leaves. The etymology of the word is derived through Latin, "from the Ancient Greek word *kaktos*, a name originally used by Theophrastus for a spiny plant whose identity is now uncertain."[105]

The only context Sophie provided for the cactus tattoo was that she experienced the impulse to get a tattoo either during or immediately after the roller derby competition. Roller derby is a physical sport involving two teams of five players, each on roller skates circling counterclockwise a flat oval track. Points are scored by a team's "jammer" lapping the opposing team's "blockers." It is known as a sport that demands mental toughness and grit.[106] Physical injuries, such as scrapes, bruises, injured knees etc., are commonplace. Sophie attested to receiving multiple injuries over the years. Roller derby is a sport where women very much control the narrative: "In much of the sporting universe, men create many of the rules, but in roller derby they do not. Instead, it is dominated by women who make the teams, drive the revenue, and they do it with a boldness they feel flips the script on what society says it means to be feminine."[107]

Looking at the image itself, there was a beautiful reddish circle behind the cactus. Symbolically, the red circle may refer to the Self, as activated and manifested from the depths of the psyche. It also suggested a sunrise component as the cactus was lit up inside with light. The green of the cactus was lush and there were two beautiful flowers growing out of the plant.

The circle was a mandala. The fact that it was red may have symbolic reference to the feeling function. The cactus was likely psychologically linked to Sophie's feeling-toned complex about hugging and being hugged. It is difficult to hug a cactus without getting hurt. The cactus spines suggested that Sophie, unconsciously

---

[105] Cactus. (2024, September 19). In *Wikipedia.* en.wikipedia.org/wiki/Cactus
[106] Roller Derby. (2024, September 24). In *Wikipedia.* en.wikipedia.org/wiki/Roller derby
[107] fairplayforwomen.com

and consciously, telegraphed to others the message not to hug her. The spines reflected the comments made by her friends that she was emotionally cold and distant. Intra-psychically, the spines represented the vulnerability Sophie felt on the feeling side and the need for her to protect that part of herself. Simply put, the spines symbolized her long-standing psychological defense system. As Jung said, mandalas are always attempts at self-healing. It was as if the Self was compensating the hugging complex with a protective circle. While offering the ego protection, the red mandala also presented the ego with the opportunity to renew itself.

The spiny cactus was a fitting symbol of this hugging complex. The spines in this context symbolized Sophie's fear of change, fear of thinking about her hugging complex, and fear of her inner world. She was comfortable with the outer world, but not the inner world of the psyche. The hugging complex is a good illustration of how we cannot relate to the world in a one-dimensional way. If we do, then even the things that we are good at become compromised. For example, Sophie's over-reliance on adapting to the world via extraversion became compromised when a social moment presented itself where hugging others and being hugged in return was the natural, feeling response of the moment. The feeling-toned complex manifested in longstanding psychological signals for others to keep their distance. When constellated, the complex prompted the ego to protect itself via the spiky cactus leaves. Sophie was a warm-hearted person who loved to laugh and socialize. However, when the feeling-toned hugging complex was constellated, it handicapped the ego to the point that even her friends, those who love her, felt her cold and emotionally distant.

It is symbolically meaningful that the cactus lives in hot and dry environments and that it is efficient at using and conserving water. The *Penguin Dictionary of Symbols* states there are three symbolic attributes associated with water: "It is a source of life, a vehicle of cleansing and a centre of regeneration."[108] Looking at the first

---

[108] Jean Chevalier and Alain Gheerbrant, *The Penguin Dictionary of Symbols* (New York: Penguin Books, 1996), p. 1081.

attribute, the source of life, one might ask: what does that have to do with Sophie? The cactus was perhaps symbolic of how her ego was compromised by the hugging complex. As a result, her ego learned to cherish and protect the water/feelings that came her way. Her parents loved her and she felt loved by them. However, like her parents, Sophie was unable to express that love via a hug or embrace. The hugging complex forced the ego to find a way to conserve and protect this vital life source by being defensive, both externally and internally.

The redeeming, cleansing aspect of water manifested in Sophie's good heart. She cared about her friends, family and the world. Her good heart was the water of life that prevented her feelings from deteriorating into bitterness. The hugging complex was a psychological stumbling block that could be resolved by conscious attention and insight.

The regenerative aspect of water shows itself in the compensatory impulse behind the tattoo. Sophie's instinctual foundation attempted to correct the situation by sending the compensatory impulse that resulted in the cactus tattoo. Sophie was a woman of integrity and strength. She exuded a lust for life and the mental toughness to engage with it. She was a survivor. This is wonderfully illustrated by the cactus tattoo and was in part related to her positive animus, which symbolically manifested in the phallic shape of the cactus. Jung affirms that one of the salient features of a woman's animus is to be the source of the spirit she lives by. Sophie lived life with gusto and spirit. This animus energy and spirit underpinned her life.

From our perspective, the image of the tattoo reflected a psychological potential for wholeness. Looking at the cactus, one got the impression of a person with outstretched arms. There was a glowing inner light, a *lumina naturae* (light of nature) that permeated the cactus. The beautiful red circle behind the cactus exuded a sense of completeness. Also, the plant/person with the outstretched arms formed a cross, the epicentre of which was the centre of the red circle. This suggested the ego's potential to approximate a sense of wholeness by establishing a conscious relationship to the Self.

It was meaningful that two blue flowers grew out of the cactus: one out of the upright column, the masculine; the other out of one of the curved arms, the feminine. A flower is a mandala image. The number two is a threshold number which suggests that some content of the unconscious is approaching consciousness. That the colour blue is often associated with the thinking function suggests that introverted thinking, which includes both the masculine and feminine, is required to unpack complexes that prevents Sophie from developing latent aspects of her personality. The image was a blueprint of Sophie's potential for wholeness.

During her twenty-fourth year, Sophie had the word CUNT tattooed under her breast on the left side. Under the word was the image of a knife. She said the knife was an embellishment by the tattoo artist, but she was okay with it. She explained that for her, the word CUNT, which refers to the vagina, had unfortunate negative connotations in the collective. However, from her own perspective, she wanted to reclaim the word in a positive sense. Again, she chose to place the tattoo under her breast as it was easy to hide. She again said she did not notice any change in her psychological attitude after acquiring the tattoo.

Tattoo 17

CUNT is considered a vulgar word for the female genitals.[109] In modern times, it has often been used to denigrate or belittle a woman or a person. According to various dictionary sources the word CUNT

---

[109] Merriam-Webster.com.

has become recognized as one of the most tabooed words in the English language.[110] However, feminists such as Germaine Greer began to change that narrative and championed the word:

Germaine Greer, the feminist writer and professor of English who once published a magazine article "Lady, Love Your Cunt" (anthologised in 1986), discussed the origins, usage and power of the word in the BBC series "Balderdash and Piffle", explaining how her views had developed over time. In the 1970s she had "championed" the use of the word for the female genitalia, thinking it "shouldn't be abusive". She rejected the "proper" word, vagina, a Latin name meaning "sword-sheath" originally applied by male anatomists to all muscle coverings—not just because it refers only to the internal canal but also because of the implication that the female body is "simply a receptacle for a weapon." But in 2006, referring to its use as a term of abuse, she said that, though used in some quarters as a term of affection, it had become "the most offensive insult one man could throw at another" and suggested that the word was "sacred," and "a word of immense power, to be used sparingly."[111]

The objective connotation of the CUNT tattoo represented the activist part of Sophie's personality which motivated her to do her part to reclaim the word in a positive sense as well as to improve quality of life for women. Sophie, being a strong-willed woman, would have objected if she did not want the knife embellishment under the word CUNT in the tattoo. Figuratively, this meant that Sophie was prepared to verbally take up arms and defend the positive connotations of the word and cleanse it of its negative connotations. She would agree with Germaine Greer that the word CUNT was sacred and to use the word in any other way was a sacrilege.

But what of the subjective meaning of the CUNT tattoo? The CUNT tattoo was the fourth in a sequential series and each tattoo in the series was meaningfully connected to the previous ones. It is important to remember that the first tattoo, the numeral sixteen, had

---

[110] *Wikipedia.* Cunt.
[111] *Wikipedia.* Cunt.

to do with birth, not only actually but symbolically as well. This had a subjective meaning given the fourth tattoo, CUNT, directly relates to the part of a woman's anatomy associated with birth. The word CUNT then, had connotations to an inner psychological birth. In addition, there is symbolic, subjective relevance to the location of the CUNT tattoo, as it is situated below Sophie's left breast. The breast has to do with the maternal, the mother. Although it was not mentioned by Sophie, the location of the tattoo was symbolically relevant to discerning its latent subjective meaning.

Sophie's admitted intention with this tattoo was to reclaim the word CUNT in a positive sense, to cleanse it of its disparaging connotations. Psychologically, this suggested she cared in a maternal, loving way about how the word CUNT had been weaponized historically to belittle and undermine women.

It is commonly known in the Jungian world that a positive life-enhancing attitude necessitates that the positive aspects of the inner feminine and masculine become integrated and work as one. When Sophie made the decision to obtain the CUNT tattoo, she was responding to an impulse from the archetypal instinctual foundation of her psyche. Because of the extraverted direction of her thoughts and feelings, she would be unconscious of the introverted connotations of the impulse. The impulse for the tattoo originated not only from the feminine aspects of the archetypes but also the masculine. If unresolved bitterness and negative thoughts towards men were present, the archetypal energies constellated and influencing the ego would affect, in a negative way, the feeling-tone of those on the receiving end. Sophie's CUNT tattoo reflected a woman with good intentions. The inclusion of the knife in the tattoo reflected an impulse from the unconscious that had positive connotations.

Before discussing the psychological implications of the knife, we need to refer to what it symbolizes when utilized in a positive way. Psychologically, the knife, like the sword, "represents a psychic function, i.e., discriminating thought and judgement."[112] The discriminating function of the knife is evident in the Grail legend and the Holy Blood of Fécamp:

> This knife is probably meant to be the same that Nicodemus used to scrape away the blood. When the blood was discovered, a small cylinder containing a piece of iron "like a part of a lance" was also found. This throws light on the particular circumstance that in Parzival the two silver knives which serve to scrape the poison from the sick Anfortas' wound when his condition is especially severe are carried in the Grail procession.[113]

> The knives, in so far as they take the place of the "broken sword" of conscious traditional thinking, certainly represent a new type of thinking which, taken from the unconscious itself, is for that reason more adequate to deal with its contents than merely conscious reflection would be. This new mental attitude would seem to be the precursor of the alchemistic turn of mind and of the psychological way of thinking which stemmed from it. It was destined to eliminate the Grail King's poisonous blood substance and, in the most literal sense, the "dried-on" blood, i.e., the no longer effective psychic essence of the Christ symbol... The thinking thus taken from the unconscious is clearly symbolized here by the two knives and is intended to protect the lance or *Imago Christi* from the desiccated residue—that is, behind the *Imago Christi* stands the Self, and what the Self attains is cultivated by a thinking achieved through self-knowledge and is thereby protected from the sterilizing effect of the intellect.[114]

When Sophie decided to take ownership of the word CUNT and reclaim it, she decided to direct her thinking function in a positive way to cleanse the word of its historical, poisonous connotations. The old King historically refers to a collective way of thinking, what von Franz would describe as an outworn and inaccurate dominant

---

[112] Emma Jung and Marie-Louise von Franz, *The Grail Legend*. (Boston: Sigo Press, 1986), p.171.
[113] Ibid., pp. 170-171.
[114] Ibid., pp. 171-172.

collective attitude with regard to the word.[115] The knife symbol within this context suggested Sophie's extraverted thinking function recognized this and wanted to rectify the situation by replacing the old way with a new dominant attitude towards the word CUNT. Sophie wanted the world to use the word CUNT with respect and love. What she was totally unaware of was that the impulse from the depths of her unconscious wanted her to do the same inwardly.

Psychologically Sophie needed to cleanse her ego of its outworn and deleterious influences, the inner poison of the old king and queen archetypes. The old King archetype manifested in a personal feeling-toned complex such as the hugging complex. It was the inertia of an attitude that compromised personal relationships by preventing a woman from embracing others and herself. Psychologically, the old Queen symbolized the feelings/eros that accompany the old dominant thinking of the King, allowing the hugging complex to remain entrenched and unchallenged within Sophie's ego. The genesis of the hugging complex was the behaviour of the parents, neither of whom embraced her or verbally told her they loved her. Hence, by psychological osmosis Sophie became what they represented, a person unable to hug herself or others. Sophie was unaware, however, that within her psyche was a masculine archetype that wanted her attention. The positive animus archetype when activated carried the potential to transmit thoughts to her ego that would change and renew this psychological impasse. The positive animus functions by transmitting healing and supportive words to the ego, i.e., saying "I love you, Sophie, embrace yourself. You are worth it." By doing so, the ego experiences an inner revival wherein the old negative attitude is replaced by a new positive one. Accompanying such words and thinking are the feelings, the eros, that go with it. This enables the ego of a woman to feel and embrace herself and others. The knife situated below the word CUNT symbolized the psychological, discriminating ultraviolet aspect of the archetype of the animus waiting to be embraced by Sophie.

---

[115] Marie-Louise von Franz, *The Interpretation of Fairy Tales*. (Dallas: Spring Publications, 1987), p. 40.

It is our contention that ultimately it was the Self that was the initiator of the impulse for the CUNT tattoo. If that is the case, we ask the question: "What was the intent of the Self with regards to the CUNT tattoo?" This question has been partially answered by our discussion of the need for Sophie to develop her undeveloped introversion, thereby developing a relationship with the inner world of her psyche. During that discussion, we have outlined the role the animus plays in establishing a relationship with the ego. The part that has not been fully discussed to this point is the role of the Self as the architect of the tattoo.

First, it must be acknowledged that the Self is a borderline concept that Jung utilizes to convey his hypothesis that there is a self-regulating, ordering, archetypal component in the depths of the unconscious. It is knowable only to a certain extent. Experience informs the ego that the Self is a mysterious, ineffable psychoid factor, operating in the depths of the psyche. Jung utilizes the term psychoid to refer to things that may exist but are irrepresentable. He wrote:

> Just as the introduction of time as the fourth dimension in modern physics postulates an irrepresentable space-time continuum, so the idea of synchronicity with its inherent quality of meaning produces a picture of the world so irrepresentable as to be completely baffling. The advantage, however, of adding this concept is that it makes possible a view which includes the psychoid factor in our description and knowledge of nature—that is, an *a priori* meaning or equivalence.[116]

Having acknowledged the ego's limitations in knowing and discussing the Self, there are still aspects of the Self that can be discerned as becoming manifest.

Previously, when discussing the implications of the ultraviolet aspect of the archetypal impulse behind Sophie's tattoos, we had suggested that from the very first tattoo there was an impulse from the Self,

---

[116] C.G. Jung, *The Structure and Dynamics of the Psyche*, Collected Works, Vol. 8, (Princeton: Princeton University Press, 1972), p. 513.

prompting the ego to initiate a conscious process of individuation. It is our position that this impulse transmitted to the ego continued with the CUNT tattoo. Basically, the Self kept prodding the ego with each impulse to commit to this psychological process. That Sophie had not undertaken such a conscious process was not surprising given her age and her emphasis on the extraverted side of life. Nonetheless, the potential remained for her to discover further psychological layers latent within the tattoo image.

It was our suggestion that the symbolic meaning latent within the first tattoo related to psychological birth and that this symbolic meaning also relates to the CUNT tattoo. The vagina is commonly referred to euphemistically as the general area "down there" which also includes the vulva, clitoris, uterus, etc. It is significant symbolically that "down there" includes the uterus, the womb, as this is the area of a woman's anatomy associated with the birth of new life. We hypothesized that when Sophie actively decided to rid the word CUNT of its poisonous cultural associations, she was unconsciously connecting to what Jung calls the positive animus. We additionally suggest that a latent meaning within the CUNT tattoo is that the knife can be utilized psychologically to open Sophie's ego to her inner world. Within this context, the knife, the positive animus, would symbolize the sperm that fertilizes the egg, the ego, resulting in the birth of an unconscious individuation process. The womb from the subjective vantage point symbolizes the archetype of the mother, the positive feminine aspect of the Self. If the positive animus fertilizes the ego, psychologically this leads to the birth of new life.

That Sophie hid her tattoos reflected an inner conflict within the ego. The ego wanted the tattoo and made the effort to get it. On the other hand, Sophie placed the tattoos in places where she could hide them as her mother did not like visible tattoos. This reflected the degree to which the ego had not fully claimed its own independence from the mother's psychological influence. If Sophie were able to tackle the hugging complex, this would mean she could claim her psychological independence from the mother.

At the age of twenty-six, Sophie experienced another impulse to get a tattoo. Her fifth tattoo was a snake and flowers tattoo on the left thigh. She stated flowers were feminine. She did not want the image to be too soft, so she included the snake, as she liked snakes. This tattoo was more visible. As with the previous ones, she said she did not notice a change in her psychological attitude after getting the tattoo.

Tattoo 18

Previously, in "Joseph's" section, we discussed the symbolism of the flower as a natural mandala representing a union of opposites, given that flowers contain both feminine and masculine parts. There were three flowers of a pinkish hue in Sophie's tattoo. One flower was fully open. Another flower was barely open while the other flower's petals were slightly more open. There were green leaves throughout the tattoo.

In 1957, Barbara Hannah gave a series of lectures which were published in book form under the title, *The Archetypal Symbolism of Animals*. In the section of the book devoted to the serpent, she distilled the vast amount of material related to it into four classifications:

1. Serpents as demons of earth, darkness and evil.
2. Serpents as spirits of light, wisdom and creativity.
3. Serpents as symbols of renewal and the *uroborus* of natural cyclic life.
4. Serpents as representing the union of the opposites and as a means of communicating with the divine.[117]

Also, Jung made the following comments about the snake in a 1929 dream seminar:

> Whenever a snake appears, it symbolizes a piece of instinctive psychology in ourselves that is simply inaccessible, something of tremendous power, a thing that is inexorable and that we cannot make compromises with. A Nordic myth says you can recognize the hero by his snake eyes, cold, not to be trusted. You can't influence the serpent thing in man, and this makes him a hero or medicine-man. The serpent in Oriental psychology is very spiritual, it symbolizes the treasure of wisdom. Yogis have an instinctive understanding of people with snake's eyes because they are in contact with that part of their own psychology. But snake's eyes of course mean the bad quality, too, something quite inhuman that you see in primitive medicine-men also. In Spencer and Gillen's book there is a photograph of such a man; he has a peculiar staring look, it is the evil eye that can charm snakes. So the hero is of a like nature. He reproduces youth by casting off his old skin and taking on a new, a continuous rejuvenation by overcoming the great dragon, Death. The inhuman quality that the snake represents is linked up with the lower centres of the brain and spinal system, into which fakirs occasionally penetrate, as when they are able to stop their own bleeding, or produce tears at will, as some actresses do; these are snake powers. When such a monstrous animal appears in a dream, we know that something is coming up from the

---

[117] Barbara Hannah, *The Archetypal Symbolism of Animals* (Wilmette: Chiron Publications, 2006), p. 165.

unconscious which is not to be influenced by will-power. It is like a fate that cannot be twisted.[118]

For this fifth tattoo, Sophie included images she liked and wanted to be affiliated with. This is the objective component of the tattoo. Now we will, again, explore the subjective component as it relates to her psychology.

The snake and flowers image was the fifth tattoo in a series. In the previous tattoo we drew reference to the birth connotations of the first tattoo and to the CUNT tattoo. That the very next tattoo was a snake and flowers tattoo suggested the symbolism of both would also be related to birth. If we pursue the idea that the fifth tattoo was related to birth, we need to ask ourselves: what is being born or at least, what wants to be born?

The snake can be seen wrapping itself around the three pink flowers. The snake's head was above the flowers and appeared to be rising. Its mouth was open with its tongue protruding. It was as if the snake was emerging and bringing the flowers with it. The leaves were even portrayed as being part of the snake's skin, as was the colour pink. This suggests the snake wanted to bring what the flower symbolized into contact with the ego. What could the flowers symbolize? We contend that the flowers represent the Self. This was suggested by the circular shape of the upper flower. Also, its beautiful petals were open and revealed a yellow inner centre. The yellow circle symbolized the opening of the inner light of the Self to the ego.

Also, as we have already seen, flowers were commonly referred to as symbols of the Self because they contain both masculine and feminine characteristics making the flower a natural mandala symbol. The pistil is the reproductive part of the flower consisting of four parts: the stigma, style, ovary and ovules. This part of the flower has been commonly referred to as the female part of the flower, as is the receptacle, the base of the flower, which holds everything in place. The stamen which is composed of two parts, the anther and

---

[118] C.G. Jung, *Dream Analysis- Notes of the seminar given in 1928-1930* (Princeton: Princeton University Press, 1984), pp. 326-327.

the filament, comprises the masculine part of the flower, as does the peduncle or stem of the flower.

We suggest the ultraviolet aspect of the archetype of the Self presents the opportunity for the ego to turn its gaze to the inner world of the psyche when appropriate. As previously mentioned, a mandala manifests psychologically when the ego is confused, disoriented and in need of protection. It was likely that the flower mandala was a compensatory response from the Self, to calm the inner anxieties accompanying Sophie's hugging and other complexes.

Earlier we referred to Hannah's four-part classification of snake images. All four seem pertinent to the psychological importance of the tattoo. The first category states that the snake represented a demon of earth, darkness and evil. We do not believe Sophie's tattoo snake symbolized a demon of earth or that it symbolized evil in this particular case. However, we do hold that part of its symbolic reality is that it is a creature of the earth and darkness. Psychologically, the earth symbolizes the instinctual aspect of the psyche and body, and the darkness suggests the snake issues from the darkness of the unconscious, instinctual foundation of the psyche.

The second category states the snake can symbolize spirits of light, wisdom and creativity. It is our position that the snake in the tattoo symbolizes all three of these aspects. The snake rising symbolically suggests it is bringing components from the unconscious depths into contact with the ego (via the skin). The components it brings are the *lumen naturae* (light of nature), the wisdom of the feminine (a positive aspect of the Self) and the creative capacity to assess the environment both outwardly and inwardly. The light of nature was the psychological light symbolized by the flower and the snake. Contained within both the flower and the snake was a reference to the feminine wisdom of the Self. The creative component was visible in the tattoo by the snake's flicking tongue and the biological function of that behaviour: instead of nostrils, snakes smell with a special organ, called the Jacobson's organ, on the roof of their mouths. Snakes use their tongues to capture smells from the environment. The flicking tongue of the snake in Sophie's tattoo symbolized the psyche's instinctual capacity to assess the ego and its mental status. If the ego were to turn its gaze inwardly and integrate what the snake's tongue symbolized psychologically, this would augment the ego's ability to assess more accurately the outer and inner worlds.

In Hannah's third category, the snake can be a symbol of renewal and the *uroborus* of natural cyclic life. The snake sheds its skin to renew itself. The ego has this snake-like capacity to renew itself by shedding its skin, i.e., by changing its attitude. The *uroborus* connotation was evident in that the snake was wrapped around the fully opened flower mandala. That it sheds its skin suggests a natural cycle of death and rebirth, in other words, out with the old and in with the new.

The fourth classification referred to the snake as representing the union of opposites and as a means of communicating with the divine. The snake's elongated body was suggestive of the masculine phallus while its winding, zigzagging movement suggested the feminine, signifying the union of opposites. The ego's responsibility was to balance itself by adopting an attitude that balanced the feminine and masculine aspects of the psyche as well as an attitude that gave due attention to both the outer and inner worlds.

But how are Jung's words quoted above relevant to the snake in Sophie's tattoo? Jung suggested that when the snake appeared, something was coming up from the unconscious that was not to be influenced by will power. He said its appearance was like a fate that cannot be twisted. This suggests the message from the unconscious to the ego was becoming more insistent, the more it was ignored. The longer Sophie remains committed to primarily adapting to the world through extraversion, the undeveloped introverted aspects of herself will become more insistent for the ego's attention.

To help us understand the insistent component of the psyche regarding the snake, we needed to once again return to the very first tattoo, the numerical number sixteen. It was symbolically significant that the first tattoo was located on Sophie's neck. Psychologically, the neck is the connecting link, the bridge between the head (the brain) and the rest of the body. From the beginning of Sophie's tattoo journey, there was symbolic reference to connecting the head with the rest of the body. We suggested from the beginning that the ego needed to open its perspective of the world to include the inner world of the psyche, the unconscious. It was extremely relevant that the tattoo Sophie obtained prior to the snake tattoo was the CUNT tattoo. The CUNT is a body part from "down there," a part of the body well below the head. However, the tattoo CUNT was a word. The symbolic significance of this is that words are what the thinking function of the ego used to assist it in understanding things. Meaning, it belonged symbolically to the head, as did the knife representing psychological discrimination. The flowers and the snake were vegetative and animal aspects of nature related to psychological understanding in a nonverbal manner. As Sophie has yet to grasp the ultraviolet meaning inherent in the tattoos prior to the snake tattoo, the unconscious has become more insistent to the ego that it establish a perspective that integrates the instinctual aspect of the psyche with the cerebral. It is meaningful psychologically that the snake and flowers tattoo was on the left thigh, as the leg is far away from the head. The leg symbolically has more to do with the instinctual foundation of the psyche.

Another symbolic facet of the snake and flowers tattoo was the numerical component. What, if any, is the psychological relevance of the fact that there were three flowers and one snake? The qualitative numerical significance of the number three and four was referenced multiple times by Jung and von Franz:

> The retrograde counting step leading from the number three to four has even been made historically famous by Maria Prophetissa's alchemical axiom. It runs: "Out of the One comes Two, out of Two comes Three, and from the Third comes the One as the Fourth." This means that the number three, taken as a unity related back to the primal one, becomes the fourth. This four is understood not so

much to have "originated" progressively, but to have retrospectively existed from the very beginning.[119]

What this suggested is the idea of unity, alluded to in the quote above, was there pre-consciously in the number one. We have already referenced this idea in the discussion of the qualitative numerical symbolism of the number sixteen tattoo. The above quote from von Franz suggests that unity was present in the three flowers but transitions qualitatively to potential realization with the fourth, the snake. The snake and flowers tattoo was a compensatory impulse from the unconscious psyche to the ego's orientation towards life. The idea of potential wholeness for the ego was evident in the very first tattoo, the numeral sixteen. That there was a prominent numerical connotation in the fifth tattoo is not a surprise but rather, as Jung would suggest, a kind of empirical evidence that numbers are a mysterious ordering component of the archetypal foundation of the psyche.

At the age of twenty-six, Sophie obtained her sixth tattoo. It consisted of a skull wearing a cowboy hat. The skull had a wheat sheaf between its teeth. There was a red scarf wrapped around where the neck would be and a similar red colour band wrapped around the crown of the hat. The tattoo was on the left side of Sophie's ribs, where it could be easily concealed. It was situated directly behind the Blinky tattoo as if the cowboy skull were looking in Blinky's direction. Sophie indicated she liked cowboy and western motifs but that there was no psychological reason for acquiring the tattoo or psychological impact after getting the tattoo. She thought she would just feel "cool" having a skull with a cowboy hat on it. This was the persona component of the tattoo.

---

[119] Marie-Louise von Franz, *Number and Time*, (Evanston: Northwestern University Press, 1974), pp. 64-65.

Tattoo 19

Before analyzing the tattoo from a subjective perspective, we will look at the symbolic connotations of some of its component parts. First, the cowboy hat merits attention. Jung suggests the hat has two psychological connotations. Outwardly it refers to a persona aspect that a person wants to be associated with. For instance, people who wear a baseball hat or another sports hat are generally signaling to others that they are a sports fan and cheer for that particular team. However, from a subjective perspective, the hat may have symbolic connotations to the larger personality within, the Self:

"… for the real personality is anything but the personal, so the person in the mask throws away the hat because the hat symbolizes the self, the total man, namely, the totality of the conscious and unconscious personality."[120]

---

[120] C.G. Jung, *Dream Symbols of the Individuation Process*, (Princeton: Princeton University Press, 2019), pp. 314-315.

Following this line of thinking, Jung suggests the hat can have mandala connotations as it is round inside and fits over the crown of the head:

"To return to our dream: The hat in this case is a mandala. This is a characteristic symbol for that strange second personality which is coming into the life of the patient."[121]

The skull also has symbolic connotations to the Self:

> The round vessel or stronghold is the skull. "The divine organ," says the *Liber quartorum*, "is the head, for it is the abode of the divine part, namely the soul." That is why the philosopher must "surround this organ with greater care than other organs." Because of its roundness, it attracts the firmament and is by it attracted; and it is attracted in similar manner by the attracter, until the attraction reaches its end in the understanding.[122]

The sheaf of wheat had similar symbolic connotations to food of a different kind, the nourishing energies and contents from the unconscious psyche:

"It is not always the fruit of the tree, but of the *granum frumenti*, the grain of wheat, from which the food of immortality is prepared as in *Aurora Consurgens* 1: 'For from the fruits of this grain is made the food of life, which cometh down from heaven'."[123]

Also, it is meaningful that Jung aligns the fish and wheat symbol when discussing rebirth. This was significant as the fish/Blinky and cowboy/wheat sheaf tattoos were in close proximity on Sophie's body:

> Where the fish disappears, there is the birthplace of *Khidr*. The immortal being issues from something humble and forgotten,

---

[121] Ibid., p. 319.
[122] C.G. Jung, *Mysterium Coniunctionis*. Collected Works, Vol. 14, (Princeton: Princeton University Press, 1974), p. 514.
[123] C.G. Jung, *Alchemical Studies*. Collected Works, Vol. 13, (Princeton: Princeton University Press, 1970), p. 306.

indeed, from a wholly improbable source. This is the familiar motif of the hero's birth and need not be documented here. Anyone who knows the Bible will think of Isaiah 53:2ff., where the "servant of God" is described, and of the gospel stories of the Nativity. The nourishing character of the transformative substance or deity is borne out by numerous cult-legends: Christ is the bread, Osiris the wheat, Mondamin the maize, etc. These symbols coincide with a psychic fact which obviously, from the point of view of consciousness, has the significance merely of something to be assimilated, but whose real nature is overlooked. The fish symbol shows immediately what this is: it is the "nourishing" influence of unconscious contents, which maintain the vitality of consciousness by a continual influx of energy; for consciousness does not produce its energy by itself.[124]

We will start our discussion of the subjective component of the cowboy tattoo by referring to the skull. The skull, as Jung remarked, was symbolically "the divine organ," the house of the soul and the conduit for the spirit, the Self. Psychologically, the skull referred to the potential for the ego to establish a relationship to the spiritual factor living within the unconscious psyche. Obviously, this was not something Sophie was conscious of when she selected the image for the tattoo. Also, we have referred to the fish/Blinky tattoo in our discussion of the skull, as it is our perspective that the third eye of Blinky symbolically referred to the ego's role of taking note of the spiritual aspect of the unconscious psyche. Both the Blinky tattoo and the cowboy tattoo were compensatory responses from the archetypal foundation of the psyche nudging the ego to develop an introverted perspective.

The cowboy hat atop the skull was symbolic of a particular psychological connotation and influence on Sophie's ego. There are two symbolic components of the word cowboy, the cow and boy. The cow as a theriomorphic (animal form) symbol has multiple connotations. Hannah lists the following four:

1. A symbol of the mother.

---

[124] C.G. Jung, *The Archetypes and the Collective Unconscious*, Collected Works, Vol. 9.1 (Princeton: Princeton University Press, 1975), p. 306.

2. A symbol of the nurturer and provider.
3. A symbol of docility.
4. A symbol of the feminine par excellence.[125]

The word "boy" was defined as: "1. A male child or youth. 2. A young man, esp. regarded as not yet mature."[126] Taking the two components of the word cowboy into consideration, what could be the subjective psychological inference of the word? As Jung remarked, the type of hat that covered the head referred to a specific psychological factor influencing the ego. Sophie specifically stated it was a cowboy hat and not a cowgirl hat, suggesting a masculine influence related to the archetype of the animus, the spirit a woman lives by. That "cow" precedes "boy" in the word cowboy suggested the degree to which the mother archetype influenced the archetype of the animus, that the two archetypes were not differentiated within her psyche. The word boy implied that the mother aspect of the psyche kept the masculine aspect in an undeveloped stage, the stage of a boy. The influence of Sophie's mother was evident in the hidden placement of the tattoos on her body, as Sophie knew her mother did not like visible tattoos. However, it is worth mentioning that Sophie wanted a more visible tattoo on one of her arms in the future. If this were to occur, it would indicate a moving away from the mother's influence. Sophie was unaware of the subjective, psychological aspects of the cowboy hat.

There was a red band or ribbon at the base of the crown of the hat with a circular shape suggestive of a mandala. The colour of the red band unconsciously suggested the feeling function. This may be related to an unconscious need to protect and encircle that function. This would be another aspect of the protective influence of the mother. Also, the red suggested a distinctly feminine character to the hat.

---

[125] Barbara Hannah, *The Archetypal Symbolism of Animals*, (Wilmette: Chiron Publications, 2006), p. 373.
[126] *The Concise Oxford Dictionary of Current English*, Ed. R.E. Allen, (Oxford: Clarendon Press, 1991), p. 133.

We now turn to the wheat sheaf clamped firmly between the skull's teeth. That the skull can clench its teeth symbolically referred to the living nature of the skull. Teeth refer to the ego's capacity to break down psychological food/material.[127] The wheat sheaf clamped firmly between the skull's teeth suggests the ego values what it symbolized, which is the potential for psychological renewal. Again, this renewal was related to the need for Sophie to develop her introversion. If this were to occur, the potential for the hugging complex to be resolved presents itself. Additionally, by consciously turning the ego's attention to the inner world, the potential exists to differentiate the animus from the mother archetype's influence. If this were to happen, the ego would mature as a result. Ultimately, the foundation for inner renewal for Sophie was based on her ego forming a conscious relationship with the centre of her psyche, the Self.

Finally, the red scarf tied around the area where the neck would be was also symbolically relevant similar to the band, as a mandala, with the red colour again likely belonging to the feeling function. The scarf gave the skull tattoo a more feminine, refined quality. This may represent the need for the ego to develop an inner attitude/feeling for Sophie's inner life. We also felt it was significant that the scarf was where the neck would otherwise be. We discussed above the symbolic connotation of the neck representing the connecting link/bridge between the head and the body. The skull tattoo represented the head, but the skull (head) was the only body part in the tattoo. The red scarf suggests the ego needs to establish a conscious bridge to the rest of the body, meaning the instinctual foundation of the psyche.

Though not a part of the tattoo, it is meaningful that horses are often associated with the cowboy and that the horse is a symbol of the instinctual foundation of the psyche. Psychologically, the ego needs to establish a good relationship with its inner horse, the instinctual

---

[127] *The Book of Symbols*, Ami Ronnberg, editor-in-chief, (Cologne: Taschen, 2010), p. 370.

foundation of the psyche. That was the ultraviolet meaning of the cowboy/skull tattoo.

Throughout the data collection interview, Sophie said there were no psychological components to any of her tattoos and she did not notice any change in her attitude after acquiring them. Therefore, we are suggesting her tattoos are a compensatory impulse from the unconscious to awaken the ego to undeveloped, introverted aspects of the personality. We have also suggested her hugging complex is evident in the tattoos, as is the need for her to develop a conscious relationship to the instinctual, archetypal foundation of her psyche.

Sophie is a dynamic, intelligent, woman who cares deeply about righting the wrongs of the world. We acknowledge and respect her strong activist spirit while also suggesting the unconscious via Sophie's tattoos is nudging her ego to become as actively engaged with her inner life, and to love that equally.

As previously mentioned, Sophie plans on getting more tattoos. She said she thinks the next tattoo would be on one of her arms, but the image had yet to be decided. We are confident her next tattoos will represent the life journey she is on, and contain unconscious responses to that life for her ego to awaken to and consider for potential integration.

Summary

The impulse to tattoo has been experienced by humans for thousands of years, and has been found throughout the world. This book came about because of our impression that the unconscious also manifests itself in the tattoos people acquire. We enlisted ten participants to provide the raw material to investigate this theory. In the chapter "Psychology and the Tattoo," we used a single tattoo from participant "Mark" to illustrate how our approach would interpret a tattoo from a Jungian perspective. This chapter is followed by three other chapters in which we interpret the tattoos of three separate individuals. It is our contention that the interpretations from a Jungian perspective related to the participants' tattoos provide compelling evidence that the unconscious manifests itself in tattoos.

Each of the participants shared their personal stories and their reasons for acquiring a tattoo. We assert that in addition to the personal, conscious reasons for acquiring a tattoo, there is an unconscious component that derives from both the personal and the collective unconscious. More specifically, the impulse to tattoo originates from the archetypal, instinctual foundation of the psyche. The unconscious component is projected by the participant's ego onto the image/skin. The archetype itself has two aspects, the ultraviolet aspect and the infrared aspect. The image of the tattoo represents the ultraviolet aspect, the mode of apprehension, the latent meaning contained within the image. The tattoo itself represents the infrared aspect of the archetype, the action taken by the individual in response to the impulse from the instinctual foundation of the psyche.

The interpretations derived from the data collected in this exploration of tattoos would not have been possible without the psychological insights obtained by Jung in his alchemical investigations. His exploration of alchemists, their work and the role projection plays in that work is the key that allowed the authors to understand how the unconscious manifests itself in tattoos. We acknowledge the gratitude we owe to this psychological trailblazer.

List of Tattoos

1) Mark's tattoo – image of family crest
2) Mary's first tattoo – image of a hummingbird
3) Mary's second tattoo – image of Mayan calendar
4) Mary's third tattoo – image of three worry dolls
5) Joseph's second tattoo – image of flower mandala
6) Joseph's third tattoo – image of a key
7) Joseph's fourth tattoo – image of five lines
8) Joseph's fifth tattoo – image of Hermes
9) Joseph's sixth tattoo – image of a red flower
10) Joseph's seventh tattoo – image of a boxer
11) Joseph's eight tattoo – image of a skull
12) Joseph's ninth tattoo – image of a diamond
13) Joseph's tenth tattoo – image of a lion
14) Joseph's eleventh tattoo – image of a warrior
15) Sophie's first tattoo – image of the number sixteen
16) Sophie's third tattoo – image of a cactus
17) Sophie's fourth tattoo – image of the word CUNT, with image of knife
18) Sophie's fifth tattoo – image of a snake with flowers
19) Sophie's sixth tattoo – image of a skull with cowboy hat and scarf

References

Books:

Allen, R. E., Ed. *The Concise Oxford Dictionary of Current English*, eighth edition. New York: Oxford University Press, 1990.

Bernt, Vicki and Lautmann, Victoria. *The New Tattoo*. New York: Abbeville Press, 1994.

Biedermann, Hans. *Dictionary of Symbolism*. New York: Penguin Books, 1994.

Bird, Mary Brave and Erdoes, Richard. *Ohitaka Woman*. New York: Harper Perennial, 1994.

Brain, Robert. *The Decorated Body*. New York: Harper & Row, 1979.

Burchett, George and Leighton, Peter. *Memoirs of a Tattooist*. London: Pan Books, 1960.

Burma, Ian and Richie, Donald. *The Japanese Tattoo*. New York: Weatherhill, 1980.

Chevalier, Jean and Gheerbrant, Alain. *The Penguin Dictionary of Symbols*. New York: Penguin Books, 1996.

Edinger, Edward. *Ego and Archetype*. Boston: Shambala, 1992.

Governor, Alan and St. Clair, Leonard. *Stoney Knows How: Life as a Tattoo Artist*. Lexington: University Press of Kentucky, 1981.

Gray, John. *I Love Mom - An Irreverent History of the Tattoo*. Toronto: Key Porter Books, 1994.

Hannah, Barbara. *The Archetypal Symbolism of Animals*. Wilmette, Illinois: Chiron Publications, 2006.

Hardy, Donald, Ed. *Sailor Jerry Collins - American Tattoo Master*. Honolulu: Hardy Marks Publications, 1994.

Jung, C.G. *Psychological Types*. Collected Works, Vol. 6. Princeton: Princeton University Press, 1971.

_____. *The Structure and Dynamics of the Psyche.* Collected Works, Vol. 8, 2nd ed. Princeton: Princeton University Press, 1972.

_____. *The Archetypes and The Collective Unconscious.* Collected Works, Vol. 9, Part 1. Princeton: Princeton University Press, 1975.

_____. *Aion: Researches into the Phenomenology of the Self.* Collected Works, Vol. 9, Part 2. 2nd ed. Princeton: Princeton University Press, 1968.

_____. *Psychology and Alchemy.* Collected Works, Vol.12. 2nd ed. Princeton: Princeton University Press, 1974.

_____. *Alchemical Studies.* Collected Works, Vol. 13. Princeton: Princeton University Press, 1970.

_____. *Mysterium Coniunctionis: An Inquiry into The Separation and Synthesis of Psychic Opposites in Alchemy.* Collected Works, Vol. 14. Princeton: Princeton University Press, 1970.

_____. *The Practice of Psychotherapy: Essays on the Psychology of Transference and Other Subjects.* Collected Works, Vol. 16. Princeton: Princeton University Press, 1975.

_____. *Dream Analysis: Notes on the Seminar Given in 1928-30.* William McGuire, Ed. Princeton: Princeton University Press, 1984.

_____. *Dream Symbols of the Individuation Process.* Suzanne Geiser, Ed. Princeton: Princeton University Press, 2019.

_____. *Memories, Dreams, Reflections.* Aniela Jaffe, Ed. London: Fontana Press, 1993.

Jung, Emma and von Franz, Marie-Louise. *The Grail Legend.* Boston: Sigo Press, 1986.

Juno, Andrea and Vale, V., Eds. *Modern Primitives: An Investigation of Contemporary Adornment and Ritual.* San Francisco: Re/Search Publications, 1989.

Krakow, Amy. *The Total Tattoo Book.* New York: Warner Books, 1994.

Ronnenberg, Ami and Martin, Kathleen, Eds. *The Book of Symbols.* Cologne, Germany: Taschen, 2010.

Rubin, Arnold, Ed. *Marks of Civilizations*. Los Angeles: Museum of Cultural History, 1988.

von Franz, Marie-Louise. *Shadow and Evil in Fairy Tales*. Dallas, Texas: Spring Publications, 1987.

_____. *On Divination and Synchronicity: The Psychology of Meaningful Chance*. Toronto: Inner City Books, 1980.

_____. *An Introduction to the Interpretation of Fairy Tales*. Dallas: Spring Publications, 1987.

_____. *Number and Time*. Evanston: Northwestern University, 1974.

_____. *C.G. Jung: His Myth in Our Time*. Toronto: Inner City Books, 1998.

_____. *The Collected Works of Marie-Louise von Franz*, Vol. 8. Asheville: Chiron Publications, 2023

Wojcik, Daniel. *Punk and Neo-Tribal Body Art*. Jackson: University Press of Mississippi, 1995.

Internet:

Wikipedia
ifcy.org
settlement.org
fairplayforwomen.com
merriam-webster.com
languages.oup.com
axiawh.com
pressconnects.com

Thesis:

Mayo, Brian. *The Relationship Between the Tattoo and The Psyche*. Zurich: C.G. Jung Institute, 1997.

Studies in Jungian Psychology
by Jungian Analysts   Quality Paperbacks
Prices and payment in $US (except in Canada, $Cdn)

The Call of Destiny: An Introduction to Carl Jung's Major Works
J. Gary Sparks ISBN 9781738738502. 10 Illustrations. Index. 192pp. $28

Sacred Chaos: God's Shadow and the Dark Self
Francoise O'Kane ISBN 9780919123656. Index. 144pp. $25

The Cassandra Complex: Living with Disbelief
Laurie L. Schapira ISBN 9780919123359. Index. 160pp. $25

Conscious Femininity: Interviews with Marion Woodman
Marion Woodman ISBN 9780919123595. Index. 160pp. $25

The Love Drama of C. G. Jung
Maria Helena Mandacarú Guerra ISBN 9781894574426. Index. 128pp. $25

The Problem of the Puer Aeternus
Marie-Louise von Franz ISBN 9780919123885. Index. 288pp. $40

Personality Types: Jung's Model of Typology
Daryl Sharp ISBN 9780919123304. Index. 128pp. $25

Live your Nonsense: Halfway to Dawn with Eros
Daryl Sharp ISBN 9781894574310. Index. 128pp. $25

Encounter with the Self: William Blake's Illustrations of the Book of Job
Edward F. Edinger ISBN 9780919123212. 22 illustrations. Index. 80pp. $25

INNER CITY BOOKS
21 Milroy Crescent.
Toronto ON M1C 4B6 Canada
416-927-0355 www.innercitybooks.net

Audiobooks

Audiobook editions of the titles below are sold directly from Amazon and other places where you buy your audiobooks. Not all titles are available from all places. Audiobooks are convenient, great for long trips, and can be a boon to those with vision impairment. Current audiobooks include these titles with many more to come:

Swamplands of the Soul
The Eden Project
Under Saturn's Shadow
  James Hollis

Addiction to Perfection
  Marion Woodman

The Call of Destiny
  J. Gary Sparks

Transformation of the God-Image
  Edward F. Edinger

~

Ebooks

ebooks are digital versions of printed books that can be purchased, downloaded, then viewed on a computer and some eReader devices. Many of our titles are available as eBooks, on our website in ePUB and/or PDF format, or from Amazon as Kindle Books.

Browse EBooks on our website below.

INNER CITY BOOKS
21 Milroy Crescent.
Toronto ON M1C 4B6 Canada
416-927-0355 www.innercitybooks.net